WHAT ARE THEY SAYING ABOUT
THE BOOK OF JONAH?

What Are They Saying About the Book of Jonah?

Rhiannon Graybill
John Kaltner
Steven L. McKenzie

Paulist Press
New York / Mahwah, NJ

Cover illustration by Julia Raketic / Shutterstock.com
Cover and book design by Lynn Else

Library of Congress Cataloging-in-Publication Data
Names: Graybill, Rhiannon, 1984– author. | Kaltner, John, 1954– author. | McKenzie, Steven L., 1953– author.
Title: What are they saying about the Book of Jonah? / Rhiannon Graybill, John Kaltner, Steven L. McKenzie.
Description: New York : Paulist Press, [2023] | Series: What are they saying about | Includes bibliographical references. | Summary: "This book provides an overview of how biblical scholars have attempted to address important issues related to the Book of Jonah"—Provided by publisher.
Identifiers: LCCN 2023016468 (print) | LCCN 2023016469 (ebook) | ISBN 9780809155583 (paperback) | ISBN 9781587689567 (ebook)
Subjects: LCSH: Bible. Jonah—Criticism, interpretation, etc.—History.
Classification: LCC BS1605.52 .G73 2023 (print) | LCC BS1605.52 (ebook) | DDC 224/.9206—dc23/eng/20230722
LC record available at https://lccn.loc.gov/2023016468
LC ebook record available at https://lccn.loc.gov/2023016469

ISBN 978-0-8091-5558-3 (paperback)
ISBN 978-1-58768-956-7 (e-book)

Published by Paulist Press
997 Macarthur Boulevard
Mahwah, New Jersey 07430
www.paulistpress.com

Printed and bound in the
United States of America

Contents

Preface

Though short, the Book of Jonah is among the best known and most loved books of the Hebrew Bible (Old Testament). The story of God's prophet and the giant fish that swallows him up is the subject of countless paintings, songs, sermons, essays, and children's art projects. The second half of the Jonah story, in which the prophet travels to Nineveh and then reacts to the sparing of the city, is also the subject of countless literary, artistic, and theological treatments. Long a favorite of readers, Jonah is also a favorite text for interpreters. Early Jewish and Christian interpreters had much to say about the Book of Jonah, from speculations about Jonah's time in the fish to allegorical interpretations of the prophet's journey to critical inquiries into the sincerity of Nineveh's repentance. Islamic sources developed their own rich set of Jonah traditions. And subsequent generations of interpreters—including modern biblical scholars—continue to study the Book of Jonah to find new ways of reading a fascinating text.

Before turning to the Book of Jonah's interpreters, it may be useful to review briefly its contents. It unfolds over four chapters. In chapter 1, Jonah ben Amittai is called by YHWH to prophesy against the great and evil city of Nineveh. Instead of doing as he is told, he flees, boarding a ship to Tarshish. The ship sets sail but is stopped when YHWH sends a storm, which only diminishes when the sailors throw Jonah overboard (with his encouragement). Jonah does not drown but is swallowed by a "great fish" (not technically a whale!). Chapter 2 takes place inside the fish, where Jonah sings a song or psalm thanking God for saving his life. The fish then spits him out. In chapter 3, Jonah at last goes to Nineveh, where he prophesies that in forty days, God will destroy the city. The people repent, and YHWH decides not to destroy them after all. Chapter 4 describes the aftermath of YHWH's decision. Jonah is extremely angry that God has shown mercy on Nineveh. He builds himself a hut to wait and see what will happen (even though YHWH has already decided). YHWH causes a plant to grow, which gives Jonah shade and pleases him greatly. YHWH then sends a worm to kill the plant and a hot wind to bother Jonah. When Jonah complains, YHWH offers an enigmatic answer, asking Jonah why he cares about the plant's welfare, but not the people and animals in the vast city of Nineveh. Then the book ends.

Recent years have seen a number of exciting developments in Jonah scholarship. In this book, we survey current work on Jonah, highlighting a handful of key issues. The first chapter surveys the composition of the Book of Jonah and how scholars say the book reached its current form. Chapter 2 considers Jonah's place in the canon, with particular focus on the "Book of the Twelve" (i.e., the twelve "Minor Prophets"), an emerging area of scholarly focus. Chapter 3 takes up the question of Jonah's genre: Is the book a satire, a prophetic tale, a parable, or something else entirely? Chapter 4 focuses on the psalm in Jonah 2, both as a stand-alone text and as it relates to the remainder of the book. The message of Jonah is the focus of our chapter 5. Chapter 6 considers some of the major interpretive questions or mysteries that still remain for readers of Jonah. And the final chapter offers a brief overview of how the book has been read by Jewish, Christian, and Muslim interpreters, as well as its influence in literature, art, and music.

We wish to thank Christopher Frechette of Paulist Press for his guidance, encouragement, and outstanding editing throughout the course of this project.

Abbreviations

AOTC	Abingdon Old Testament Commentaries
AT	Authors' Translation
AuOr	*Aula Orientalis*
AYB	Anchor Yale Bible
BCE	Before Common Era
Bib	*Biblica*
BTCB	Brazos Theological Commentary on the Bible
BZAW	Beihefte zur Zeitschrift für die alttestamentliche Wissenschaft
CBC	Cambridge Biblical Commentary
CBQMS	Catholic Biblical Quarterly Monograph Series
CE	Common Era
ConBNT	Coniectanea Biblica: New Testament Series
ConcC	Concordia Commentary
ConcJ	*Concordia Journal*
CTJ	*Calvin Theological Journal*
EBR	*Encyclopedia of the Bible and Its Reception*
Hist.	Herodotus, *The Histories*
ICC	International Critical Commentary
JBL	*Journal of Biblical Literature*
JHebS	*Journal of Hebrew Studies*
JPSBC	Jewish Publication Society Bible Commentary
JQR	*Jewish Quarterly Review*

JSOTSup	*Journal for the Study of the Old Testament Supplement Series*
LHBOTS	Library of Hebrew Bible/Old Testament Studies
MT	Masoretic Text
NICOT	New International Commentary on the Old Testament
NRSV	New Revised Standard Version
OTL	Old Testament Library
RB	*Revue biblique*
SEÅ	*Svensk exegetisk årsbok*
SHBC	Smyth & Helwys Bible Commentary
SymS	Symposium Series
VT	*Vetus Testamentum*
VTSup	Supplements to Vetus Testamentum
WBC	World Biblical Commentary

1
How the Book of Jonah Took Shape

Who wrote the Book of Jonah? The most common view about Jonah's composition today is that it was the work of a single author. The second most common view is that it is a unified work except perhaps for the psalm in chapter 2, which was added later. In older scholarship, though, theories of multiple writers behind the book were typical, despite the book's small size—just forty-eight verses in all. Such theories have persisted especially in Europe and are now beginning to regain popularity. While their details vary, these theories posit either two or three levels of composition in the book, and they follow one of two models: a block model, whereby a version of chapters 3—4 constitutes the oldest part of the book and chapters 1—2 were added to them; and a layer model, in which there are layers throughout the prose narrative.

Our reconstruction of Jonah's composition shares perspectives with both models. We agree that the psalm in Jonah 2 is an addition to the prose story, and we think that the psalm had its own developmental history distinct from the prose. We discuss that history in chapter 4. Within the prose story are inconsistencies that suggest it developed in two main stages: an original story that is mostly preserved in chapters 3—4 and a subsequent editorial revision or redaction that significantly enlarged and reshaped that story. There are also a few minor glosses that probably began as marginal additions that worked their way into the text. In what follows we offer our own translation of the prose story of Jonah (i.e., without the psalm in chapter 2). In order to indicate what we think are its compositional layers, we present the original story in standard font, additions by the reviser in *italics*, and scribal glosses in curly brackets {}. The location of the psalm is indicated by square brackets.

The Composite Story of Jonah[1]

1 [1] Jonah the son of Amittai received the message from YHWH that said, [2] "Get up and go to Nineveh, the great city, and cry out against it, because its evil has come to my attention." [3] So Jonah got up

to flee to Tarshish, away from YHWH. *Going down to Joppa, he found a ship heading to Tarshish. He paid the fare and boarded it to travel with them to Tarshish, away from* YHWH. [4] *But* YHWH *hurled a strong wind at the sea, creating a powerful storm, and the ship had a mind to break in pieces.* [5] *The sailors were afraid so that each of them cried out to his god(s). They hurled the ship's cargo into the sea to lighten it. Meanwhile, Jonah had gone down into the hold of the vessel and had fallen fast asleep.* [6] *The captain came to him and said, "What are you doing asleep? Get up and cry out to your god! Maybe god will notice us so that we won't die!"* [7] *They said to each other, "Come on, let's cast lots to find out whose fault it is that this disaster is upon us." When they cast lots, the lot fell on Jonah.* [8] *They said to him, "Tell* us {who's responsible for this disaster we're experiencing.} *What is your occupation? Where are you from? What is your country, and of what people are you?"* [9] *He said to them, "I am Hebrew, and I worship* YHWH *the God of heaven who made the sea and the dry land."* [10] *The men were terrified and said to him, "What have you done?!" For the men knew that he was fleeing from* YHWH {because he had told them.} [11] *They said to him, "What should we do with you so that the sea will stop raging against us?"—because the sea was becoming increasingly stormy.* [12] *He replied to them, "Pick me up and throw me into the sea so it will stop raging against you, because I know that it is because of me that this powerful storm is against you."* [13] *The men tried to row back to dry land, but they could not, because the sea was becoming increasingly stormy around them.* [14] *They cried out to* YHWH *and said, "O* YHWH, *don't let us die for this man's life, and don't blame us for innocent blood. For you,* YHWH, *do as you please."* [15] *So they picked Jonah up and threw him into the sea, and the sea stopped its raging.* [16] *Then the men were terrified of* YHWH. *They offered a sacrifice to* YHWH *and made vows.* [17] YHWH *appointed a great fish to swallow Jonah and Jonah was in the fish's belly three days and three nights.*

2 [The psalm occurs here in 2:1–9]

[10] YHWH *commanded the fish and it vomited Jonah onto dry land.*

3 [1] *Jonah received the message from* YHWH *a second time:* [2] *"Get up and go to Nineveh, the great city, and cry out to it the message that I tell you."* [3] *So Jonah got up*

and went to Nineveh as YHWH commanded.

(Nineveh used to be an enormous city—three days' walk across.)

[4] Beginning to enter the city *one day's walk*, Jonah cried out "Forty days more and Nineveh is overturned." [5] The people of Nineveh believed in God and called for a fast, dressing in sacks from the greatest of them to the least.

[6] *Word reached the king of Nineveh, who got up from his throne, removed his royal robe, donned a sack, sat in ashes,* [7] *and issued a proclamation: "In Nineveh, by order of the king and his high officials, let not human or animal,*

cattle or sheep taste anything or graze or drink water. ⁸
Let them cover themselves—both humans and animals—
with sacks."

They cried out fervently to God, and each and every one of
them repented from their evil ways and from the violence
that was in their hands, saying, ⁹ "Who knows whether
God will change his mind and turn from his anger so that
we will not die?" ¹⁰ God saw what they did, changing
from their evil ways, so God changed his mind about the
evil intended for them and did not do it.

4 ¹ *This struck Jonah as a terrible idea, and it made him*
angry. ² *So he prayed to* YHWH, *"Oh* YHWH, *this is*
what I thought when I was in my country, isn't it? This is
the reason I fled toward Tarshish before—because I knew
you to be a gracious and merciful God, slow to get angry,
very kind, and changing your mind about bringing harm. ³
Now, YHWH, *take my life from me, because I'm better off*
dead than alive!" ⁴ YHWH *said, "Is it right for you to be*
angry?"

⁵ Jonah went out from the city and sat down to the east of it.

He made a shelter for himself there and waited in its shade

until he could see what would happen with the city. ⁶
YHWH God appointed a plant that grew up over Jonah to
give shade to his head {to save him from his discomfort},
and Jonah found great joy in the plant. ⁷ God appointed a
worm at dawn the next day, and it attacked the plant so that
it dried up. ⁸ Then when the sun arose, God appointed an
oppressive east wind. The sun bore down on Jonah's head
until he became faint

and asked to die, saying "I'm better off dead than alive!"
⁹ *God said to Jonah, "Is it right for you to be angry about*
the plant?" He replied, "I am right to be angry—enough
to die!"
¹⁰ YHWH said, "You cared about the plant which you
did not cultivate or grow, which came about in a night and

died in a night. [11] So I should care about Nineveh, shouldn't I—that great city, in which there are more than 120,000 people who don't know their right from their left, *not to mention many animals?*"

Explanation

The original version of the book was a simple tale about Jonah's successful mission to Nineveh that read as follows:

> Jonah the son of Amittai received the message from YHWH that said, "Get up and go to Nineveh, the great city, and cry out against it, because its evil has come to my attention." So Jonah got up and went to Nineveh as YHWH commanded. Barely entering the city, Jonah cried out "Forty days more and Nineveh is overturned." The people of Nineveh believed in God and called for a fast, dressing in sacks from the greatest of them to the least. They cried out fervently to God, and each and every one of them repented from their evil ways and from the violence that was in their hands, saying, "Who knows whether God will change his mind and turn from his anger so that we will not die?" God saw what they did, changing from their evil ways, so God changed his mind about the evil intended for them and did not do it. Jonah went out from the city and sat down to the east of it until he could see what would happen with the city. YHWH God appointed a plant that grew up over Jonah to give shade to his head and Jonah found great joy in the plant. God appointed a worm at dawn the next day, and it attacked the plant so that it dried up. Then when the sun arose, God appointed an oppressive east wind. The sun bore down on Jonah's head until he became faint. YHWH said, "You cared about the plant which you did not cultivate or grow, which came about in a night and died in a night. So I should care about Nineveh, shouldn't I—that great city, in which there are more than 120,000 people who don't know their right from their left.

This initial tale illustrated the principle of "reciprocal repentance" described in Jeremiah 18:7–8: "At one moment I may declare concerning a nation or a kingdom, that I will pluck up and break down and destroy it, but if that nation, concerning which I have spoken, turns from its evil, I will change my mind about the disaster that I intended to bring on it." The Ninevites repented of their evil deeds because of Jonah, and YHWH in turn repented of the destruction threatened against the city. The ending (4:10–11) implied by a rhetorical question that compassion for the people of Nineveh was YHWH's motivation for lifting the city's punishment. Since it presupposed the Book of Jeremiah, this tale was probably written in the Persian period (ca. 539–333 BCE).

A second writer revised and expanded this story into a very different kind of work. The reviser added the story of Jonah at sea in chapter 1 by taking its opening in a surprising new direction. In other stories, prophets respond to YHWH's call by doing exactly as they are told. So, in 1:2 when God tells Jonah to "arise and go," one expects to read that he "arose and went."[2] Verse 3 starts as expected by saying that "Jonah arose." But the next word is not "and went" as expected but rather "to flee." It is not until 3:3, after YHWH repeats the directive, that Jonah "arose and went to Nineveh according to YHWH's word." This is an instance of "narrative resumption" (also known by its German name *Wiederaufnahme*). Authors and editors employ such a technique to rejoin a narrative after a detour (for an author) or an insertion (by an editor). There are several indications that this repetition is editorial and was used to insert the story in Jonah 1. The most important of these is that the characters and events in chapter 1 are adapted from Hellenistic Greek literature. Such is not the case for chapters 3—4, suggesting that chapter 1 originated later than the other two chapters.

The Greek parallels are: (1) a musician named Arion is rescued by a dolphin after Corinthian sailors steal his money and force him overboard;[3] (2) a vase painting depicts the hero Jason being disgorged by a sea monster while the goddess Athena looks on; (3) Herakles (Hercules) rescues the princess Hesione by allowing himself to be swallowed by a sea monster, which he then kills from inside; (4) Perseus kills or turns to stone a sea monster that devoured Andromeda, daughter of Queen Cassiopeia.

These parallels account for certain features of Jonah 1 that are otherwise puzzling. For instance, Jonah's rescue by the fish is a combination of roles played by the dolphin in the first parallel and the sea monster in the other three. Its real function in Jonah is neither to rescue nor to threaten Jonah but to provide a "do-over" for him to fulfill YHWH's commission. Similarly, the sailors in Jonah are an adaptation of the Arion story. They are not villains like the Corinthians but correspond to the Ninevites in chapter 3 in their pious response to the storm and their attention to Jonah. Their role in throwing Jonah overboard is a remnant of the Greek motif of the evil foreign sailor, since it is not entirely appropriate for Jonah, who could have jumped. Another such remnant is the captain in Jonah, who disappears after his brief appearance in 1:5b–6. His cameo is due to the mention of the captain as the leader of the sailors in variants of the first parallel. Finally, the Hellenistic tales account for the mention of Joppa as Jonah's port of departure. It was not the closest port to Jonah's hometown of Gath-hepher in Israel (2 Kgs 14:25), and in the eighth century BCE when the story of Jonah is set, Joppa was not under the control of either Judah, where it was located, or Israel. Its mention is a leftover influence of the myth of Perseus and Andromeda, which was associated with Joppa from the fourth century BCE on, thereby indicating the Hellenistic period (ca. 333–64 BCE) as the most likely time of the story's reviser.

Besides the Greek parallels, other features indicate that chapter 1 was added later. Except for 4:2 (also editorial), chapters 3—4 show no awareness of the events of Jonah 1. In addition, inconsistencies between chapter 1 and chapters 3—4 indicate that they were not always a unified story. For example, in 1:5 Jonah boasts that he is a Hebrew who worships YHWH, while in chapters 3—4, he does not identify his ethnicity or the God for whom he speaks, even when he delivers his prophecy in 3:4. Also, in 1:16 the sailors offer sacrifices after the sea has calmed, while the Ninevites do not sacrifice in the midst of their crisis or afterward. Finally, the logical point for YHWH to repeat the command to Jonah to go to Nineveh is while Jonah is inside the fish when the futility of his escape attempt is obvious and he must listen. The delay till Jonah is back on land accommodates the insertion of the story in 1:3–17.

The original story continued in 3:3 with the statement that Jonah went to Nineveh as YHWH commanded. The reviser's hand surfaces again in verse 3 in the description of Nineveh as an enormous city. Here the reviser enhances the usual description of Nineveh as a great city by adding two phrases—"to God" and "three days' walk across." "To God" is not always translated literally, because it is probably an idiomatic way of expressing superlative meaning, in this case "extremely large" or "ginormous, humongous."[4] The hyperbole signals the hand of the reviser. "Three days' walk across" gives an idea of the dimensions that the reviser imagines for Nineveh. It would be about forty-five to sixty miles (three times fifteen to twenty miles), roughly the diameter of the larger Dallas–Fort Worth metroplex. It is an exaggeration of extreme proportions, since no city in the ancient Near East was anywhere close to that size.

The statement in 3:4 that "Jonah began to enter the city, a day's walk" is confusing, since going a full day into a city's interior is more than beginning to enter it. The "one day's walk" presupposes the previous measure of a three-day walk for the diameter and is, therefore, also from the reviser. The original story probably envisioned the city gate of Nineveh as the place where Jonah delivered his prophetic oracle. This makes sense culturally, since the gate was where business was customarily transacted in ancient Near Eastern cities (Gen 23:10, 18; 34:20, 24; Deut 21:19; 22:15, 24; 25:7; Isa 29:21; Amos 5:10, 12, 15; Ruth 4:1, 10–11). It also fits with Jonah's attitude; he doesn't want to be there, so he does the bare minimum. The rest of verses 4–5 also belongs to the original story. Jonah utters his very brief and opaque prophecy, which nonetheless moves all of the population to repentance.

The anecdote in 3:6–9 farcically portrays the king as lagging behind his people by ordering them to do what they are already doing. His inclusion of the animals is part of the farce, since they cannot fast, dress themselves, or repent. The king's edict in verses 6 and 7, and the first clause of 8 was added by the reviser (another *Wiederaufnahme* that picks up with the reference to sackcloth). The original account described the people's repentance in verses 4–5 and verses 8 (after the mention of sacks) and 9. (See the keyed translation).

God's decision to spare Nineveh in 3:10 was part of the original story, and it was followed by the notice in 4:5 that Jonah went to a spot east of the city to wait and see what would happen to it. God did not communicate his decision to Jonah but instead used the occasion as a teaching moment. Jonah's angry reaction in 4:1–4 was the reviser's addition. It contradicts 4:5, where Jonah does not know what will happen to Nineveh, and it assumes chapter 1. It also shares in the absurd picture of Jonah as a prophet whose mission is completely successful and yet who is upset "to death" about God's merciful response. The reference to Jonah building a booth in the middle of 4:5 is either an editorial addition or a scribal gloss. The repetition ("sat east of...sat under") is yet another *Wiederaufnahme*. It makes the shade plant in the next verse unnecessary. The motive for it is uncertain but perhaps related to the Jewish festival of Booths or Sukkot (Lev 23:34–44; Deut 16:13–16).

Most of 4:6–11 comes from the original story. The gloss in verse 6 may have been intended to account for the plant after the booth. Jonah's request to die and the follow-up in 4:8b–9 resemble the reviser's work in 4:3. The final reference to many animals in 4:11 recalls their involvement by the reviser in 3:6–8. The word "great" in verse 11 and also in verse 6 may also be the reviser's additions.

Conclusion

In agreement with the recent resurgence of older theories on Jonah's composition, we theorize that the book began as a simple story of Nineveh's repentance in response to Jonah's proclamation and God's reciprocal decision not to destroy the city. That story is preserved in the very beginning of the book and in sections of Jonah 3—4. However, the story was greatly expanded and revised by the addition of the story of Jonah's attempted flight in chapter 1 and by layers added to chapters 3—4. The psalm in chapter 2 was also added at some point. In the rest of this book, we will explore multiple facets of the fascinating book that resulted from this compositional process.

2
Jonah's Place and Role in the Canon

In both the Jewish and Christian Bibles, Jonah is found among the prophetic books. In the Jewish canon it is part of the Book of the Twelve, a section of the Hebrew Bible comprised of a dozen relatively short works that are each identified by the name of the prophet who is either its purported author or somehow associated with it (Hosea, Joel, Amos, Obadiah, Jonah, Micah, Nahum, Habakkuk, Zephaniah, Haggai, Zechariah, and Malachi). In the Christian ordering of the Bible these twelve books are listed separately and are commonly referred to as the Minor Prophets to distinguish them from the lengthier prophetic writings of Isaiah, Jeremiah, and Ezekiel.

Since the last decade of the twentieth century, Jonah's role in the Book of the Twelve has been a topic of increased interest and debate among Bible scholars. In other words, the book's "place" as a prophetic book is secure and well established, but in recent times certain questions have emerged about the role it plays in the subset of prophetic works within which it is found. In particular, the Book of Jonah has figured prominently in attempts to understand the relationships among the writings that make up the Book of the Twelve, especially issues regarding the order of the works, the evidence of editorial activity within them, and the shared terminology and

11

thematic elements they contain. The contours of that scholarly discussion will form the basis of this chapter.

A Point of Order

An intriguing aspect of the Book of the Twelve is that the works that comprise it are not always found in the same order in ancient manuscripts. The ordering listed in the previous section is the one that is found in Hebrew manuscripts, sometimes referred to as the Masoretic Text (MT). But some of the oldest and most important manuscripts of the Greek translation of the Hebrew, known as the Septuagint, preserve an alternative order in which Jonah occupies the sixth position rather than the fifth, and the works both before and after it are in a different sequence (Hosea, Amos, Micah, Joel, Obadiah, Jonah, Nahum, Habakkuk, Zephaniah, Haggai, Zechariah, and Malachi). This variation has led to differing views among scholars regarding which order might be the original one and whether it is even possible to determine if there was an original fixed sequence to the Book of the Twelve.

The views of James D. Nogalski and Marvin A. Sweeney demonstrate the range of scholarly opinions on the matter. On the one hand, Nogalski believes the MT ordering of the books is older and holds this view for literary reasons.[1] He posits a series of intricate connections that exist within the Book of the Twelve in the form of shared phrases and catchwords (i.e., shared vocabulary) that unite adjacent works in the collection. Because the MT arrangement better preserves these connections, Nogalski believes it reflects the original order of the books. Furthermore, his analysis proposes an interesting aspect of Jonah's role within the Twelve: its placement between Obadiah and Micah in the MT interrupts and cuts off the shared vocabulary that exists between those two books, which suggests that Jonah was a later addition to the Hebrew version of the Book of the Twelve. Many scholars concur with Nogalski's opinion that Jonah was perhaps the last work added to the Twelve.

Sweeney, on the other hand, favors the Greek order of the books for reasons that are tied more to historical contexts. He maintains that through its ordering the Greek tradition shows concern for the fate of the Northern Kingdom of Israel, while the Hebrew sequence reflects more of an interest in the Southern Kingdom of Judah and Jerusalem. This suggests the chronological priority of the Greek order because the Northern Kingdom was invaded and came to an end prior to the Southern one.[2] Similar to the approach that Nogalski takes, Sweeney also points to vocabulary connections between the Books of Jonah and Nahum to support his case because Nahum follows Jonah in the Greek ordering. For example, the opening verse of Nahum refers to Nineveh, a city mentioned in the last verse of Jonah.

One might think that the Dead Sea Scrolls could help settle the matter regarding which order of the Book of the Twelve is the original one because they are the oldest biblical manuscripts that have been discovered. Unfortunately, that is not the case due to the fragmentary nature of the scrolls. The oldest known copy of the Twelve, from approximately 150 BCE, is missing its beginning and ending portions, but the manuscript clearly indicates that the Book of Malachi, which is otherwise always the final book of the Twelve, comes before the Book of Jonah in it. This has led some scholars to propose that the scrolls show evidence of a different order of the Twelve from the one that was eventually canonized. Others have rejected this idea because the entire manuscript has not been preserved and it is possible that it contained only some of the Book of the Twelve and not the entire set of books. Consequently, the question of whether the Hebrew or Greek order of the Twelve is older remains unresolved.[3]

Jonah among the Twelve: Linguistic Considerations

Scholars disagree on whether the Book of the Twelve is a unified collection of works that was likely edited by a redactor who gave it its final shape. Ehud Ben Zvi believes this is not the case and prefers to view them as separate books because writers in antiquity often brought together and anthologized disparate works that did not have much in common. Additionally, he notes that throughout history communities and groups have often considered the Twelve to be an anthology and not a coherent collection.[4] This can be seen, for example, in the Christian canon, where the books are listed separately and lack a formal heading that groups them together as the Jewish canon does. Another reason why Ben Zvi rejects the idea that the Twelve is a single collection is the fact that each of the books begins with a superscription that serves as an introduction to the work that simultaneously sets it off from the book that comes before it. For example, the opening verse of Micah reads, "The word of the LORD that came to Micah of Moresheth in the days of Kings Jotham, Ahaz, and Hezekiah of Judah, which he saw concerning Samaria and Jerusalem," clearly indicating a break after the Book of Jonah that precedes it in the Hebrew ordering. It should also be noted that the genre of Jonah supports the position that the Book of the Twelve lacks literary unity because it is the only one that is written in prose (except for the prayer-psalm in chapter 2, which is generally held to be a later addition to the book).

At the same time, scholars have noted certain links between some of the books in the Twelve that suggest redactional activity that was meant to connect them, and this is the dominant view. This can be seen in Nogalski's observation, mentioned above, that particular catchwords and phrases found in adjacent books serve to unite them. At the same time, however, Nogalski does not find many such connections between Jonah and the works that precede and follow it in the MT. This point favors the view commonly held by scholars cited earlier that Jonah was likely the last work added to the Book of the Twelve. If the catchwords are the result of redactional work, the evidence suggests that such activity took place prior to the time that Jonah was added to the collection. In her analysis of the texts, Diana V. Edelman has determined that words related to six different Hebrew roots are found in both the last chapter of Jonah and the first chapter of Nahum, a finding which suggests to her that the order of the Twelve in the Greek translation is more original than that of the Hebrew.[5]

Another attempt to argue for unity in the Book of the Twelve can be seen in the work of Aaron Schart, who claims that Jonah's genre of satire challenges and ridicules the view of other nations that is found in the Book of Joel.[6] The total destruction of the nations is foretold in Joel 3, but in Jonah the opposite happens as the inhabitants of Nineveh are spared. He also finds vocabulary echoes between the two books. For example, in Joel 2:14 the Israelites are asked a rhetorical question that challenges them to have faith in God: "Who knows whether he will not turn and relent, and leave a blessing behind him, a grain-offering and a drink-offering for the LORD your God?" This is similar to what is said in Jonah 3:9, only there it is spoken by the people of Nineveh. Schart maintains that the Jonah passage echoes the one in Joel to critique the latter's xenophobic perspective. These linguistic and thematic connections between the two books suggest to Schart that Joel should be read with Jonah in mind and that the latter work challenges the former's exclusionary view of foreigners. It is therefore interesting to see how the genre of Jonah can be appealed to in support of both the idea that the Book of the Twelve is a unified entity and the opposite view that there is no discernible connection among the works it contains.

Perhaps the most elaborate argument for redactional activity within the Book of the Twelve has been put forward by Jakob Wöhrle, who sees connections among several of the writings that are all based on the passage in Exodus 34:6–7a: "The LORD, the LORD, a God merciful and gracious, slow to anger, and abounding in steadfast love and faithfulness, keeping steadfast love for the thousandth generation, forgiving iniquity and transgression and sin." Wöhrle refers to this as the "Grace Formula," and parts of it are found most fully in Jonah 4:2 and Joel 2:13, with Micah 7:18–19, Nahum 1:2b–3a, and Malachi 1:9a also containing vocabulary from it. He argues that this creates a complex structure in which the Grace Formula gives order to the Book of the Twelve since it is present in books at each end of the collection and in three books in the middle. According to Wöhrle, Jonah is the theological center and focus of the framework because its first three chapters contain examples of human repentance and divine forgiveness through the experiences of the sailors (chapter 1), Jonah (chapter 2), and the people of Nineveh (chapter 3). This is followed by an example of God's willingness to forgive in chapter 4.[7]

Schart has expressed opposition to Wöhrle's analysis and believes that the presence of the Grace Formula in these books can be explained in a less complicated fashion, particularly where it is found in its fullest forms in Joel and Jonah. He appeals once again to his idea that Jonah is a satire, and he maintains that the book is simply mimicking what is found in Joel in order to belittle and ridicule that book's exclusivist view of foreign nations. Klass Spronk has also criticized Wöhrle's work because it disrupts the unity of the Book of Jonah, and he does not think the presence of the Grace Formula in the Book of the Twelve is significant since its complete form is present seven times in the Hebrew Bible as well as twenty additional times in a shortened form.[8] Wherever one lands on the question of whether the Book of the Twelve is a unified whole, it is clear that Jonah has played an important role in discussions of the matter.

Jonah among the Twelve: Thematic Considerations

In addition to the evidence provided by shared vocabulary, paying attention to themes that are prevalent throughout the Book of the Twelve can provide much insight into the connections and relationships that exist among the works in the collection. Edelman has carefully engaged in this type of analysis and has come up with a list of thirteen themes in Jonah that are found in at least one other book of the Twelve. She reminds us that we should not read too much into this shared material, since many of these themes are in direct contradiction with what is said elsewhere in the Twelve.

In other words, certain sections of Jonah both affirm and challenge the messages found in the other books. In this way, Edelman and others believe that Jonah can serve as an interpretive key for the entire collection. In order to limit our discussion here, we will briefly consider four themes identified by Edelman that are found in at least one-half of the books of the Twelve including Jonah.[9]

The first theme is the honoring and worshipping of YHWH by foreign peoples and nations. This is present in Jonah in the scenes describing the actions of the sailors in chapter 1 and the Ninevites in chapter 3, where both groups acknowledge the power of Jonah's God and engage in ritual activities directed toward his deity. Similar expressions of honor toward YHWH are found elsewhere throughout the Book of the Twelve, as seen in Malachi 1:11: "For from the rising of the sun to its setting my name is great among the nations, and in every place incense is offered to my name, and a pure offering; for my name is great among the nations, says the LORD of hosts" (cf. Mic 4:1–4; Zeph 2:11; 3:8–9; Zech 8:22–23).

A second theme is YHWH's involvement in the affairs of other nations, which is dramatically displayed in how the Ninevites' offenses are forgiven in the fourth chapter of Jonah. In other parts of the Twelve YHWH shows a similar interest in and influence over what takes place in foreign lands, as seen for example in Zephaniah 3:6: "I have cut off nations; their battlements are in ruins; I have laid waste their streets so that no one walks in them; their cities have been made desolate, without people, without inhabitants" (cf. Amos 9:7; Obad; Nahum; Mal 1:1–5). An important difference between how Jonah addresses this theme compared to other books is that YHWH shows a capacity for mercy and compassion toward Nineveh that is usually not found in interactions with foreigners elsewhere in the Twelve.

The importance of following the law is a third theme that Edelman finds often present in the Twelve. This is seen in a number of ways in the Book of Jonah. When the prophet refuses to heed the initial divine call to go to Nineveh, he is punished through the sending of the storm and his imprisonment in the fish until he finally acquiesces. His final words inside the fish mention the prayers, sacrifices, and vows he offers toward the deity (2:7–9). In addition, the so-called Grace Formula that Jonah utters in 4:2 calls attention to the mercy, compassion, and forgiveness that those who remain faithful will experience. The fate of those who fail to do so is described in Zechariah 7:12: "They made their hearts adamant in order not to hear the law and the words that the LORD of hosts had sent by his spirit through the former prophets. Therefore great wrath came from the LORD of hosts" (cf. Hos 4:6; Amos 2:4; Hab 1:4; Zeph 3:4; Mal 2:6–9).

The final theme to mention is the idea that YHWH relents under certain conditions and does not inflict the threatened punishment. This is, of course, most obviously seen in the Book of Jonah in the decision to refrain from punishing the Ninevites in 3:10. Here, too, what sets Jonah apart is that virtually all the other examples of similar divine mercy in the Twelve are directed toward Israel, as seen in Hosea 11:8–9:

> How can I give you up, Ephraim? How can I hand you over, O Israel? How can I make you like Admah? How can I treat you like Zeboiim? My heart recoils within me; my compassion grows warm and tender. I will not execute my fierce anger; I will not again destroy Ephraim, for I am God and no mortal, the Holy One in your midst, and I will not come in wrath. (cf. Amos 7:3–6; Joel 2:13–14; Zech 1;17; 8:14)

As noted before, the most significant difference between Jonah and the other books of the Twelve is its more positive view of foreign nations. This is most clearly seen when we compare Nineveh's fate as a city that is saved in Jonah with its complete destruction in the Book of Nahum (2:8–3:7). This indicates that Jonah holds a different view on a topic that many of the books have in common: how God treats foreigners. From this perspective, Jonah expresses the minority view on an issue that is a concern throughout the Book of the Twelve. This suggests that Jonah plays a more important role than simply being an add-on to the collection after the rest of it had been compiled. Rather, it voices a dissenting opinion on a significant issue as it introduces into the Book of the Twelve the possibility that other nations can experience divine mercy.

Conclusion

Jonah has been at the center of many of the scholarly debates and discussions involving the Book of the Twelve. Why the MT and the Septuagint present different orders of the collection remains a mystery, but Jonah has been at the heart of those conversations. The book has also figured prominently in questions surrounding the unity of the Twelve. The vocabulary and thematic connections within the works are discernable, but do they completely negate the view that the Twelve is simply an anthology of separate works? The proposed Grace Formula in particular highlights the need to evaluate the evidence judiciously. Its fragmentary form (i.e., one or two words) in some of the books of the Twelve coupled with its fuller presence in other biblical books raises issues about the claim that it serves to unite the collection. Perhaps the idea that Jonah's presence within it helps to promote a conversation within the Book of the Twelve offers the most fruitful way for understanding its place within the collection. As we've seen, a key element of that conversation is YHWH's relationship with and concern for foreign nations.

3
The Genre of Jonah

Among the most contested issues in the scholarly study of Jonah is the question of the book's genre. *Genre* is a term that comes from literary criticism; it refers to the larger category to which a work of literature belongs. Understanding genre correctly helps us to be better readers: a story about a woman who is swallowed by a wolf sounds different whether we are reading a news article or a fairy tale. For many biblical texts, genre is relatively clear: Genesis 1 and 2 are creation myths; most of Genesis 12—50 is legend; the Books of Samuel and Kings contain a mix of history, legend, and other literary forms. Psalms are a widely recognized biblical genre; they can also be categorized with more specificity. For instance, a psalm of lament sounds different than a psalm of thanksgiving. Prophecy is another broad genre category that contains a number of subcategories, including call stories (in which a person is called to be a prophet), oracles, and sign acts (in which prophets perform symbolic actions, e.g., Ezek 4–5 or Jer 13).

But what is the genre of the Book of Jonah? Scholars have offered a number of answers to this question. We will survey the most common, significant, and persuasive answers before offering our own thoughts below.

Jonah as a Satire or a Parody

It is frequently proposed that the Book of Jonah is intended as a humorous work of literature—more specifically, a satire or a parody.[1] Satire is a form of derisive humor directed at a specific target (which may be a person, a nation, or humanity as such). Literary theorist M. H. Abrams stresses that unlike comedy, "satire 'derides'; that is, it uses laughter as a weapon."[2] The goal of satire is to comment on social or genre conventions. In recent times, satire has become a dominant form of cultural humor; websites such as The Onion and television programs such as *The Office*, *The Simpsons*, and *South Park* are among well-known examples. A parody is a subset of satire that imitates specific details in order to make a humorous point. A parody is traditionally literary, although music, television, and film also offer significant examples. Alexander Pope's "The Rape of the Lock" and Jonathan Swift's "A Modest Proposal" are satires, while Seth Grahame-Smith's novel (and Burr Steers's film) *Pride and Prejudice and Zombies* and the musical stylings of "Weird Al" Yankovic are parodies.

Many elements suggest that the Book of Jonah is a work of satire. The protagonist, Jonah, is in many ways a ridiculous character, from his hasty flight from YHWH to his pompous posturing before the sailors and captain on the ship to his absurd and unnecessary anger in chapter 4. That he spends nearly all of chapter 2 inside a fish adds to the ridiculousness of his plight. Other details add to the satirical feel, including the extreme piety of foreigners (first the sailors, then the Ninevites), the clothing of animals in sackcloth and their participation in the fast, and the significant narrative roles played by such lowly actors as a worm and a *qiqayon* plant in chapter 4.

Why would a satire target Jonah? Often, scholars suggest that the book represents anti-prophetic satire.[3] By satirizing Jonah as a bad prophet, the authors or editors of the text also suggest how a prophet *ought* to act (i.e., the opposite of how Jonah acts!).[4] It is not universally accepted, however, that the book's target is prophecy, even by those who accept that Jonah is satirical. John Miles argues that the real target of the book is the excessive piety of some returning exiles from Babylon following the exile.[5] The Book of Jonah pokes fun at their rigidity through the overly rigid character of Jonah. Arnold Band further develops this argument.[6] Another possibility is that the text satirizes Jonah's narrow ethnic worldview and his inability to imagine God showing mercy to non-Israelites.[7]

Other readers seek to link Jonah to specific literary genres of satire or parody. André LaCocque and Pierre-Emmanuel Lacocque develop a lengthy argument that the Book of Jonah is a Menippean satire, though their argument has largely been neglected or rejected by others.[8]

Jonah as a Prophetic Tale

A second possibility is that the Book of Jonah represents a prophetic tale or story about the life of a prophet. Interpreters who argue for this possibility often point out that similar examples occur in both the Hebrew Bible and other related literature. The Books of 1–2 Kings, for example, contain quite developed narratives about the prophets Elijah and Elisha, along with other stories about the *benei nebiim* or "sons of the prophets." With these parallels in mind, Jonah's story can also be cast as a series of prophetic adventures. Fleeing from God, spending time in a fish, and successfully prophesying to a heathen city are notable feats. Several specific textual details also connect Jonah with Elijah and Elisha. Jonah ben Amittai, the prophet's full name, appears in 2 Kings 14:25, and a midrashic tradition associates Jonah with the son of the widow of Zarephath, whom Elijah brings back to life. Jonah's anger at God in chapter 4 also recalls Elijah's anger at God in 1 Kings 19:4; both prophets express their anger as extreme enough to die.

Jonah's adventures in chapters 1 and 2 also have the feel of a tale intended to entertain and amaze as much as to instruct.

As we discussed in the previous chapter, the account of Jonah being swallowed by the giant fish is related to Hellenistic seafaring tales. And the time in the fish (and the language of descent in the psalm in chapter 2) resembles the hero's journey to the underworld, a familiar narrative pattern. Inanna/Ishtar, Enkidu, Persephone, Odysseus, Orpheus, and Aeneas are among the many who make this journey. The Christian tradition of the Harrowing of Hell is another related example (the parallel is amplified by Jesus's own references to the "sign of Jonah" in two of the four Gospels[9]).

Postbiblical tradition often emphasizes the same features of the Book of Jonah that suggest the text is a prophetic tale. Jewish midrashic texts such as *Pirqe Rabbi Eliezer* and the *Mekhilta of Rabbi Ishmael* amplify and expand upon Jonah's adventures; in the former text, for example, Jonah tours the depths of the sea from inside the fish, peering out through its eyes while riding in it much like a submarine. And in the Islamic "Stories of the Prophets" (Arabic, *qiṣaṣ al-anbiyā'*), Jonah is a well-developed character. The text includes some elaborations that add to the overall narrative development, including Jonah bringing his entire family to Nineveh and the fish transporting Jonah to the "Coral Castle" before casting him out on the banks of the Tigris River.

Jonah as Midrash, Parable, or Didactic Story

Some interpreters agree that the Book of Jonah is fundamentally a story but disagree that its purpose is to entertain or amaze. Instead, they suggest that Jonah is didactic literature—that is, literature intended to teach or instruct. Jonah is not just a prophet who amuses us; his story teaches us a lesson. Thus Julius Bewer, for example, calls Jonah "a story with a moral," an assessment that many subsequent interpreters have shared.[10]

Often, interpreters who classify the text in this way will identify a specific genre that the Book of Jonah is said to resemble. One such genre is midrash (pl. midrashim), a form of Jewish biblical interpretation that embellishes or expands upon the often-terse biblical narrative, generally in the service of larger theological or interpretive points. The suggestion that the Book of Jonah is a midrash is made, for example, by Phyllis Trible in her influential literary study of the book.[11] Sometimes, the identification of the text as a midrash is accompanied by further speculation on what it is a midrash *on*. (Generally, a midrash uses one biblical text or character to comment on another; the midrashim on the Book of Jonah, such as *Midrash Jonah*, are not principally concerned with making points about Jonah.). Trible suggested that Jonah was a midrash on Exodus 34:6, "The LORD passed before him [Moses], and proclaimed, 'The LORD, the LORD, a God merciful and gracious, slow to anger, and abounding in steadfast love and faithfulness.'" Discussed in chapter 2 as the Grace Formula, this phrase is, of course, echoed by Jonah himself in 4:2. Others identify the book as a midrash on Jeremiah 18:7–10, representing "a test that articulates YHWH's freedom to act in judgment or salvation toward any nation."[12]

Another possibility is that Jonah is a parable, a *mashal*, or a didactic story.[13] A parable is a simple story that illustrates a lesson. In the case of Jonah, the lesson is often taken to be about forgiveness or about God's universal mercy, which Jonah fails to comprehend. The reader, however, grasps what Jonah himself cannot. Janet Howe Gaines, for example, argues that the book is about forgiveness.[14] We discuss these issues further in chapter 5, which takes up the message of Jonah. Another related possibility is that Jonah is a *mashal*, a Hebrew word often translated as "proverb" but also used for short didactic stories, parables, and allegories. In postbiblical Jewish literature, the *mashal* is a common form of rabbinic instruction that occurs widely in midrash. It is sometimes argued that Jonah represents an earlier biblical iteration of this interpretive strategy.

It is tempting to identify the Book of Jonah with these existing genres. However, closer analysis reveals difficulties. The ways that modern scholars use terms such as *midrash* and *parable* often do not fully map onto ancient understandings. As Jack M. Sasson points out, a classic *mashal* or parable has a strict rhetorical form that the Book of Jonah does not follow; specifically, a *mashal* consists of "an anecdote followed by its own explanation," known in Hebrew as the *nimshal*.[15] However, this clarifying explanation is lacking in Jonah. And two key features of a Menippean satire—an unreliable narrator and authorial self-parody—are missing in Jonah as well.[16] Still, it is possible to argue that the Book of Jonah best fits in the genre of didactic literature, even if it varies from some of the most common forms this literature takes.

Other Possibilities

There are still other possibilities for the genre of Jonah. Judson Mather suggests that the comedy of the book is best understood as burlesque.[17] Literary theorist Terry Eagleton describes the book as a surrealist farce.[18] Roger Syrén, meanwhile, calls it a "reversed diasporanovella," a short story that ends with diaspora and displacement from home.[19] And older interpreters have often read the book allegorically or typologically. Many Christian Church fathers, including Jerome, Tertullian, and Ambrose of Milan, interpreted Jonah as a type of Christ, with Nineveh representing the Church. A second strand of allegorical interpretation, traceable to Augustine, identifies Jonah as representing Israel and/or the Jews. Such allegorical interpretations continued into the medieval period and beyond. Father Mapple's sermon on Jonah in Herman Melville's *Moby-Dick* offers a famous literary example, casting the story as an account of the challenges of following God's will.[20]

Another intriguing possibility concerning genre comes from Ehud Ben Zvi, who suggests that the Book of Jonah is intended as a text that teaches us how to read. By using familiar genre features from other prophetic literature, the Book of Jonah becomes a sort of meta-instructional manual "devoted to issues that are of *relevance for the understanding of the messages of other prophetic books*."[21] This suggests that the authors of Jonah are consciously using genre.

Conclusion

As this chapter has aimed to make clear, no scholarly consensus exists about the genre of the Book of Jonah. Nearly everyone agrees that the book *has* a genre; just what that genre is, however, is debated. We tend to agree with those of our colleagues who read the book as a satire, particularly in its final form. There is certainly humor in the way that Jonah is portrayed, as well as in many of his adventures. However, we would suggest that the analysis of genre should be paired with an analysis of the text's history. At different points in its history of composition, the Book of Jonah reflects different genres. The oldest layer of the text, which includes Jonah in and after Nineveh but not chapters 1—2, most closely resembles the prophetic tale. The material that is added in chapter 1 shows the influence of Hellenistic seafaring adventure stories, just as chapter 2 is clearly a psalm of thanksgiving. The resulting final text most closely resembles a satire.

Like some of our colleagues,we are more interested in what the discussions about genre illuminate about the text, and about literature more broadly, than we are in determining a final answer.[22] Genre is just one tool to help us understand the text.

4
Jonah's Psalm

As suggested in our discussion in chapter 1, the psalm in Jonah 2 interrupts the prose story, which flows well without it. In this chapter we will discuss the composition of the psalm as well as the psalm's artistry and its role in the complete book. Before exploring the psalm, however, we must note an oddity concerning verse numbering, which differs slightly between the Hebrew (MT) text and the NRSV translation. Chapter and verse numbers were not inserted into the book until centuries after the text was finalized, and this was not done uniformly. The NRSV text includes the verse about Jonah being swallowed by the fish as the last verse of the first chapter (1:17), but the Hebrew Bible makes it the first verse of the second chapter. Consequently, between the two versions the verse numbering disagrees by one, for example, Jonah 2:1 NRSV is Jonah 2:2 MT, and so on. The discussion here will use the NRSV versification.

The Composition and Role of the Psalm in Jonah

Perhaps the most debated question in the academic study of Jonah has been the relationship of the psalm to the prose narrative. Until about fifty years ago, the widespread assumption was that the psalm was a later addition, but opinions now seem to be more or less evenly divided. There are several considerations.

The psalm does not fit well with the portrait of Jonah and his situation in the prose story. It mentions the sea but not the fish, nor the sailors, nor any of the events of chapter 1. The psalm is a psalm of thanksgiving for divine rescue (vv. 2, 6, 9), but Jonah is still inside the fish. Even if he is no longer in danger from drowning, he does not know what will happen to him. Besides, the psalm does not fit his character—he is not the thankful type. Moreover, there are differences in terminology; the most curious of these is that the fish changes gender. The masculine form of the noun is used for the fish that swallows and vomits up Jonah (1:17; 2:10), but the introduction to the psalm uses the feminine form (2:1). (The question of the fish's gender is treated in more detail in chapter 6.) There are some other notable differences in word usage as well. The word *great* is repeated frequently in the prose but does not occur in the psalm. The psalm uses a different word for "throw" (2:3) than the one found in the story (1:12). The psalm uses the plural "seas" (2:3) instead of the singular "sea," which consistently occurs in the prose (1:4, 9, 11, 12, 15). The psalm also uses the expression "from the eyes of" (2:4) instead of "from the face of" as in the prose (1:3, 10).

Other differences are more contradictory in nature. The psalm (2:3) blames YHWH, rather than the sailors, for throwing Jonah into the sea, and instead of running away from YHWH, the psalmist was driven away (2:4). The concern to see the temple again (2:4) is appropriate to someone from Judah, since the temple was in Jerusalem, but not to Jonah, who is from Israel (2 Kgs 14:25). The anti-idol sentiment in the psalm (2:8) clashes with the depiction of the sailors and the Ninevites, who do not give up their gods. The psalm concludes with the promise to offer sacrifices (2:9) but without any mention of obeying YHWH and going to Nineveh.

These inconsistencies and contradictions indicate that the psalm and the prose story were written by different authors, but not that the psalm was written later. A preexisting psalm could have been incorporated by the author of the prose because it mentions the sea, drowning, and the like. (In our view, this "author" would have been the reviser who added the story in chapter 1.) The incorporation of psalms into the mouths of characters in stories is fairly common in the Bible, as for example in the song of Hannah (1 Sam 2:1–10), which is a precedent for the song of Mary in the New Testament (Luke 2:46–55). It is not unusual even today to recall a word or phrase or idea from a song even in circumstances that are very different from those envisioned or addressed by the song.

Even if the same author who added the story in chapter 1 could have added the psalm, consideration of the way the psalm changed the Book of Jonah as a literary work strongly suggests that it was added later. The flow of the story improves greatly if the reader skips over the psalm (2:1–9) and goes straight from the mention that Jonah was in the fish for three days and nights (1:17) to YHWH's command to the fish to vomit Jonah out (2:11). It also becomes evident that the prose story has two symmetrical halves, with the sailors and their captain on the ship in chapter 1 balanced by the Ninevites and their king in the city in chapter 3.

Another consideration in favor of the psalm as an insertion is its own multilayered composition. While not commonly recognized by scholars, this is indicated by two tensions between verse 7 and other parts of the psalm. The statement in verse 7 that the author remembered YHWH and prayed at this point disagrees with verse 3, according to which the psalmist cried out to YHWH from the start. Verse 7 also portrays this moment as the low point when the author's "life" (*nephesh*; probably better rendered "spirit," conveying courage, enthusiasm) was about to fade away. Yet the previous verse concludes with the notice that YHWH has already rescued the psalmist.

In part because of these inconsistencies, some interpreters have understood the poem as a random collection of lines and formulas borrowed from the Psalms.[1] But its tight structure, especially in verses 2–3 and 5–6, counters that theory. On the basis of parallels in ancient Hebrew and Ugaritic poetry, we believe that these verses (minus "he said" in v. 2) represent the older level of the psalm, which we reconstruct in our translation below.[2] (We have lettered the line pairs or bicola for the convenience of reference.)

> A [2] I called out to YHWH in my distress,
> > and he answered me.
> B From the bowels of Sheol I cried out for help;
> > you heard my voice.
> C [3] You threw me into the heart of Sea;
> > River surrounded me.
> D All your breakers and waves
> > passed over me.
> > (Verse 4)
> D' [5] The waters encompassed me to my neck/life;
> > Deep surrounded me.
> C' Extinction was bound to my head.
> > [6] At the bases of the mountains
> B' I descended into the underworld,
> > Its bars behind me forever.
> A' You brought my life up from the pit,
> > O YHWH my God.

The original poem was one of praise to YHWH for rescue from a desperate crisis. It consisted of two quatrains (A–D and D'–A'), with four bicola of two parallel lines each. The two quatrains combined are chiastic, meaning that the lines correspond to one another from the outside in. Thus, YHWH's name appears in the first and last lines of the poem, which also mention rescue. "Sheol" (the place of the dead) in B corresponds to "underworld" in B', and both depict confinement. "River" in C and "extinction" in C' are both alternative titles for the deified Sea. "Heart" and "head" in these two bicola are both body parts. Bicola D and D' both describe sinking and the threat of drowning and thereby move the focus from sea to death. The possible dual meanings of these two words contribute to this combination of water and death in the image of drowning. The word for "neck" or "life" (*nephesh*) in D′ captures the threat of being engulfed. The word translated "extinction" in C′ is at once both "sea reeds" (*suph*) and "end" (*soph*) in Hebrew.

The poem's date is uncertain, but it shares features with older poetry that suggest that it may well come from the time of the monarchy (ca. 1000–586 BCE). This would make it the oldest portion of Jonah.

The original psalm, though, was revised by additions in verses 4 and 7–9. Inserted in the original poem's center, between D and D′, verse 4 reads:

> I thought, "I have been driven out from your presence,
>   How will I again look at your holy temple?"

These lines do not follow the neat parallelism of the original poem. They are difficult to render as poetry and could also be construed as prose. They contain none of the water imagery of the older poem and even interrupt the continuity of that imagery between verses 3 and 5. They shift to a more parochial focus in which YHWH's presence is identified with the temple in Jerusalem and thus change the theme from personal crisis to the crisis of the Babylonian exile in 586 BCE.

Appended after the conclusion of the original poem (A′), the other addition, verses 7–9, reads:

> [7] As I grew faint,
>   I remembered YHWH.
> My prayer came to you
>   at your holy temple.
> [8] Those who guard worthless lies
>   abandon their loyalty.
> [9] But with a grateful voice
>   I will sacrifice to you.
>   I will pay what I have vowed;
>   salvation belongs to YHWH!

We have already discussed the tensions between verse 7 and the earlier poem. The verse also repeats the phrase "at your holy temple" from verse 4, a further indication that it is secondary. In verse 8 "worthless lies" is an expression for idols. The denunciation of idol worshippers here, while completely foreign to the older poem, goes along with the emphasis on worship in the temple in verses 4, 7, and 9. Similarly, sacrifice and the payment of vows in verse 9 are activities that took place in the temple. The language of these latter two verses is common in the Book of Psalms and suggests that verses 4 and 7–9 were added together in order to adapt the original poem into a psalm suitable for liturgical use in the temple community.

The psalm, then, was written in two stages, both of them independent of the two-stage writing of the prose story. Whoever added the psalm introduced it in 2:1 and left a clue about the addition in changing the fish's sex. The motive for the addition was most likely the image of drowning in the sea, which seemed appropriate to Jonah's situation before the fish swallowed him. The image is a metaphor, like our own expression "drowning in debt," but elaborated by the psalm.

The Literary Artistry of the Psalm

Whatever the psalm's developmental history, it stands in the Book of Jonah as a finished product, and we can treat it as such in considering its craft. Its poetry is so complex and sophisticated, in fact, that it requires analysis in several different categories.[3]

Persons and Speaker

The poem alternates between the psalmist (in the first-person) as subject (vv. 2, 5b, 7, 8, 9) and as object (4, 5a, 6). But even as subject, he is remarkably passive. He is *acted upon* by the waters, then by YHWH. His only actions are almost all vocal: calling out for deliverance and offering praise. YHWH, addressed

in the second person except in verses 2a and 9b, saves the psalmist but is also the cause of his suffering, having cast him into the
water and banished him from the temple.

Structure

The psalm begins and ends with mentions of YHWH,
forming an envelope construction.[4] Several interpreters have
suggested that its structure is a chiasm.[5] As indicated above, the
original poem was chiastic. Verse 4 was added to it exactly in the
middle, suggesting that the reviser adapted the original chiasm to
a new focus on being driven from the temple.

Parallelism

The psalm exhibits parallelism, the hallmark of Hebrew
poetry, especially in verses 2–5. Thus, the opening two bicola in
verse 2 correspond in meaning, while artfully varying the order of
their elements:

> I called out to YHWH in my distress,
>   and he answered me
> From the bowels of Sheol I cried out for help;
>   you heard my voice.

The items in the second line also elaborate or amplify those in the
first: "I called out to YHWH" parallels "I cried out for help"; "in
my distress" is amplified by "from the bowels of Sheol"; "and he
answered me" corresponds to "you heard my voice."

In 2:3 parallelism occurs *within* each bicolon:

> You threw me into the heart of Sea;
>   River surrounded me.
> All your breakers and waves
>   passed over me.

"Sea" matches "River," and "your breakers" matches "your waves."

Verse 4 is difficult to divide into bicola, which is one reason for considering it secondary:

> I thought, "I have been driven out from your presence,
>   How will I again look at your holy temple?"

But its two long lines still display parallelism in "your presence" and "your holy temple." The first line supplies the basis (being driven out) for the psalmist's worry about never seeing the temple again.

Parallelism reveals an obvious bicolon in the first part of verse 5:

> The waters encompassed me to my neck/life;
>   Deep surrounded me.

"Waters" and "deep" are a pair, as are "encompassed" and "surrounded."

There is uncertainty about how to scan the rest of verses 5 and 6. We continue the scheme of bicola:

> Extinction was bound to my head
>   6 At the bases of the mountains.
> I descended into the underworld,
>   its bars behind me forever.

But it is possible to read the two verses as two tricola:

> 5 The waters encompassed me to my neck/life;
>   Deep surrounded me.
>   Extinction was bound to my head.
> 6 At the bases of the mountains,
>   I descended into the underworld,
>   its bars behind me forever.

Either way, the double meaning of "extinction/reeds" is in play in a transition from water imagery to death. The synonymous parallelism of the previous lines gives way to "synthetic" parallelism, which does not "repeat" the same idea but expands on it. As a result, the psalm gathers speed in these lines and hastens to a climax in:

> But you brought my life up from the pit,
> > O YHWH my God.

The continuation of the psalm (v. 7a) might suggest that it was during rescue that the psalmist remembered YHWH.

> As I grew faint,
> > I remembered YHWH.

This and the remaining bicola in verses 8–9 are in synthetic parallelism, as each adds an act of praise to the psalmist's response: prayer, confession, sacrifice, oath.

> 7b My prayer came to you
> > at your holy temple.
> 8 Those who guard worthless lies
> > abandon their loyalty.
> 9 But with a grateful voice
> > I will sacrifice to you.
> I will pay what I have vowed;
> > salvation belongs to YHWH!

Imagery

The imagery in the psalm is predominately aquatic: heart of Sea, River, breakers, waves, waters, Deep, and reeds (extinction). The references to Sea, River, and Deep, which are variously paired in Ugaritic poetry, suggest a mythic level of signification (cf. Job 38). The Sea had cosmological significance, with the mountain of the chief god El standing at the confluence of the cosmic waters. The Sea imagery, thus, evokes primeval chaos and the undoing of YHWH's ordered creation. Jonah's expulsion onto "dry land" recalls Genesis 1:9 and hints that Jonah experiences "re-creation." The fish's belly is a sort of womb, so that Jonah's recreation is also a rebirth.[6] The water imagery shared with the "Song of Moses" in Exodus 15:1–13 reinforces the understanding of Jonah's psalm as thanksgiving for salvation, just as God delivered Israel from bondage in Egypt.

The threat to Jonah is not envisioned as slavery but death, and a secondary set of images in the psalm concerns death and the underworld: Sheol, extinction, underworld, and pit. Cosmologically, the entrance to the underworld and Death's abode was at the base of the mountains (2:6), where Sea also converged. In Jonah's psalm, it is portrayed as a walled city whose gates are barred to prevent not intrusion but escape. Elsewhere in the Hebrew Bible, Sheol is paired with the bottom of the sea (Amos 9:2–3) and is imagined to swallow its victims (Ps 141:7; Prov 1:12), much as the fish does Jonah.

Body images constitute a third significant group. "Bowels of Sheol" mixes the reproductive and the digestive. It is balanced by the heart of Sea in the next bicolon (2:4). The psalmist's own body comes to the forefront at the very moment it approaches death. His throat and head are threatened and by extension his life, as is clear when YHWH brings up the speaker's life (a different word from "neck") from the underworld. The vulnerability of the body is figured again in 2:8, where the speaker describes himself growing faint.

Finally, the psalm includes multiple images related to worship. The introduction describes the psalm as a prayer. The psalm itself twice mentions the temple or sanctuary (vv. 4, 7), as well as the acts of sacrifice and payment of vows, which were performed in the temple (2:10). Meanwhile, it denounces idol worship (2:9).

Movement

Spatial theory is a relatively new approach in biblical studies that focuses on spaces in texts and the movements within and between them.[7] Jonah's movement in chapter 1 is downward—to Joppa, into the ship's hold, and then into the sea. The psalm continues this same progression, as the psalmist experiences sinking, described as water encompassing and passing over him with foliage/extinction wrapped around his head (vv. 3, 5). Verse 6 uses the verb "descend" for the psalmist's entry into the underworld, which is literally underground according to the assumed cosmology. YHWH's intervention in verse 6 reverses the direction by raising the psalmist up from the underworld. The worship activities in verses 7–9 subtly continue the upward movement with prayers and sacrifices directed to YHWH above.

Conclusion

Despite its independence from the prose story, the psalm adds a great deal to the book. It provides a pause for the characters and readers to reflect and reset. More than that, it displays Jonah's humanity and raises theological questions that are important for the book as a whole. Perhaps above all, the psalm expresses the sense of terror of a person who feels that their very existence is threatened and that their situation is hopeless. It is a human trait in times of crisis to look for comfort and assurance in language and images that are familiar and part of the sufferer's traditions. There is comfort in acknowledging God's control over sea and dry land (1:9), including its creatures, like the fish. The reader sympathizes and shares the sense of relief and gratitude when deliverance comes at the end. But one can also understand Jonah's lingering sense of anger at God, which explodes in 4:1–3, for making him endure such an ordeal in the first place. Thus,

Jonah's psalm hints at a difficult theological question that lies at the heart of the book: the Why of God's ways. Why does God consign Jonah to the fish—to punish him, to save him, or both? Why does God who is in control of the cosmos and individually manages its elements and inhabitants (fish, plants, worms) permit and even cause suffering? Why did God forgive the Ninevites only to use them later to brutally destroy his own people Israel? It is typical of the Book of Jonah to raise such questions but leave them open for the reader to address.

5
The Message of Jonah

While biblical scholars often deal with short units of text (typically a chapter or less), they generally treat the book as a whole when discussing Jonah's message. The prose narrative (chs. 1, 3, and 4) typically receives more attention than the poem, and the book's final chapter is given special significance. Its meaning is quite contested, and the mysterious ending invites further reflection and debate. Because the final scene of Jonah is so important to the question of message, it is worth revisiting. First God causes a plant to grow, which pleases Jonah greatly (4:6). God then destroys the plant and sends an oppressive east wind, which infuriates Jonah (4:7–9). The book ends with God's words:

> YHWH said, "You cared about the plant which you did not cultivate or grow, which came about in a night and died in a night. So I should care about Nineveh, shouldn't I—that great city, in which there are more than 120,000 people who don't know their right from their left, not to mention many animals?" (4:10–11; AT)

The book does not provide an answer to this question, though interpreters have offered many of their own, often linking them to arguments about the book's meaning or message. In tracing some lines of interpretation related to Jonah's message, we will comment on how these interpretations understand God's question and its meaning.

An Argument for Universalism

Interpreters of the Book of Jonah commonly suggest that the book is fundamentally about the struggle between universalism and particularism. In this framework, the character of Jonah represents the individual or particular, while YHWH, who graciously forgives the Ninevites and spares their city from destruction, symbolizes the universal. The book's key theme of the universality of God's power first appears in chapter 1, in Jonah's conversation with the sailors. Asked to identify himself, he describes himself thusly: "I am Hebrew, and I worship YHWH the God of heaven who made the sea and the dry land" (1:9; AT). However, despite his lofty pronouncement and insistence on God's broad power over sea and land alike, Jonah is ultimately too small-minded to see beyond his own individual experiences and identity, particularly his identity as an Israelite. This explains his anger at God's choice to forgive Nineveh: The prophet is afflicted with ethnic chauvinism and unable to care about the fate of the Other. YHWH's lesson to Jonah with the plant and the worm in the final chapter is a lesson about looking beyond the particular to the universal. The answer to the question of whether God should care about the fate of Nineveh and its many inhabitants is, from this perspective, clearly *yes*.

Reading Jonah's message as a call for universalism clarifies several of the hermeneutic challenges that the Book of Jonah poses. Chapter 4 contains several perplexing events: Jonah's initial anger, the puzzle of YHWH's final question, and Jonah's outburst that includes the Grace Formula: "I knew you to be a gracious and merciful God, slow to get angry, very kind, and changing your mind about bringing harm" (4:2; AT). These events are fitted into a larger framework of meaning in which Jonah represents the small, petty, and ultimately incorrect particularistic worldview, while YHWH represents the universal. Identifying universalism as the book's key message also helps connect the chapters to each other; the piety of the foreign sailors in chapter 1 and of the foreign Ninevites in chapter 3 now fit nicely with Jonah's lesson from God in chapter 4. Even the psalm in chapter 2 can be read as contributing to this message, if we consider its general focus on deliverance and the refusal to limit salvation to a specific sort of person or ethnic group (this reading becomes stronger if we understand the reference to the temple in 2:8 as a later addition).

Perhaps unsurprisingly, readings that treat the Book of Jonah as an argument for universalism are often implicitly or explicitly Christian in their orientation. Christianity's focus on the universal, set forth as early as Paul's letters (e.g., Gal 3, Rom 1—3), makes this reading of Jonah's message easily available to Christian interpreters.[1] Compassion, mercy, and forgiveness are often singled out as values by these interpreters. In the way he treats the Ninevites, God shows the importance of these values for all people. Compassion and mercy are to be valued above all else, and not limited to one's own faith community; as God forgives, so too should we forgive.

A Caution against Antisemitic Reading

The interpretations we have discussed above—universalism, mercy, compassion, divine freedom (and limited human understanding)—have much to commend them. But as astute critics have pointed out, they also risk sliding toward antisemitism if readers are not careful. Much of this has to do with the role that the character Jonah plays in these interpretations, whether as a bad example or as a foil to the divine. In their enthusiasm for the book's purported message, interpreters sometimes present Jonah as parochial, petty, or unable to grasp divine forgiveness and mercy. The trouble arises when this understanding of Jonah's character is coupled with a reading that treats him as a representative of Judaism or the Jews, juxtaposed to an (implicitly Christian) God or set of divine values. Jonah becomes the caricature of the rigid Jew who fails to understand Christian mercy. Tracing this line of interpretation, Yvonne Sherwood has aptly diagnosed its tacit (or sometimes explicit) supersessionism (the idea that Christianity fulfills and replaces Judaism) and antisemitism.[2]

Unfortunately, treating Jonah as a "small-minded Jew" is an interpretation with a long history. Antisemitic treatments of Jonah are already present in Augustine (354–430 CE) and further developed by Martin Luther (1483–1546 CE), who harshly criticized Jonah for his failure to accept universal divine mercy.[3]

In raising these concerns, we are not suggesting that the Book of Jonah should not be read as a treatise on mercy, forgiveness, or universalism. Neither do we find the figure of Jonah above criticism, including for his failure to understand God's actions and will. What we do offer is a plea for sensitivity and attentiveness in how we construct our readings of the book.

A Struggle between Justice and Mercy

If Christian interpreters incline toward compassion and universalism in their readings of Jonah, Jewish interpreters most frequently view the book as being about the problem of justice. At the heart of this reading is God's decision to spare Nineveh, which represents not simply a city of foreigners but rather Israel's "archenemy" and "destroyer."[4] Nineveh was the capital of Assyria, the powerful and brutal empire responsible for the destruction of the Northern Kingdom of Israel. Why would God spare such a people, knowing that they will destroy Israel, his chosen people? Do they deserve God's mercy, or does even mercy have its limits? From this perspective, the book exemplifies what Uriel Simon identifies as the "primordial struggle between justice and mercy."[5] The tradition of reading the Book of Jonah aloud in the synagogue on the afternoon of Yom Kippur (the Day of

Atonement) underscores the importance of its questions of justice and mercy.

The struggle between justice and mercy is a common theme in rabbinic Jewish hermeneutics; the rabbis describe God's two hands as the hand of mercy and the hand of justice. Mercy must sometimes be restrained for justice to be done; according to some midrashim, God ties back the hand of mercy to allow the hand of justice to act.[6] In a similar struggle in the Book of Jonah, the prophet represents justice, while God's actions represent mercy. Or, alternatively, Jonah's act of protest can be interpreted as an attempt to forestall God's judgment of Israel and thus the work of justice. According to *Mekhilta of Rabbi Ishmael*, Jonah resists prophesying to the Ninevites because he fears that they will repent and God will then use them against Israel (e.g., Isa 10:5).[7] This also explains why Jonah flees: he hopes that by leaving Israel, he will interrupt God's call, because the deity does not reveal himself outside of Israel).[8]

A Demonstration of Divine Power and Incomprehensibility

For other interpreters, the central message of the Book of Jonah is about divine power. The book repeatedly demonstrates that God is powerful and acts as he wishes, in ways that may transcend human understanding. Unlike human ability, divine power has no limits.[9]

Taking the book's key message as one of divine power allows us to acknowledge the significance of forgiveness and compassion in the book while expressing our own discomfort or dissatisfaction with these themes. Like Jonah, we may struggle to accept God's choice to forgive Nineveh. In fact, God's ability to forgive and Jonah's failure to do so can be understood as signaling the gap between human frailty and limitless divine power. Thus, the Book of Jonah is about divine power as well as divine incomprehensibility.[10] God shows mercy because God is *free to show mercy*—and to do whatever else. God's actions may be incomprehensible to our human selves (another common idea in many Christian theologies). This divine freedom can exceed ordinary understanding, because, according to this interpretation, *God is free not to be understood by us.* Thus, mercy and compassion in Jonah are important in their own right, but also for what they show us about the nature of God.

A Commentary on Environmental Care

Recently, several interpreters have shown an interest in the environmental, ecological, or animal-oriented values at the heart of the Book of Jonah.[11] For a book of its length, Jonah contains a remarkable number of animals: the fish in chapters 1 and 2, the penitent animals of Nineveh in chapter 3, and the worm/larva in chapter 4. The natural world is also quite significant, including the storm in chapter 1 and the plant, sun, and wind in chapter 4. And, of course, the final words of the book are "and many animals," suggesting their importance to the text and beyond it.

Environmental and ecological readings take several forms. Often, ecologically minded interpreters suggest that the message of universalism in the book extends not just to other human beings but to all God's creatures. The book aims to teach not religious tolerance but an ethic of care for creation. This is reinforced by God's actions with the plant and his final words to Jonah, which focus on care and on the nonhuman living world.

More recently, interpreters have also directed attention to the role of animals in the book. Animal studies has emerged as an important subdiscipline in biblical studies, and animals clearly play central roles in Jonah. Animal-oriented readings delve into the complex relationships between human and nonhuman creatures, often exploring what Donna Haraway has termed "companion-species" relationships.[12] As readers seek a deeper understanding of humans and animals in the Hebrew Bible, Jonah is a promising text to explore.

An Unclear Message

Finally, some interpreters suggest that the Book of Jonah does not communicate a clear message at all. Literary-oriented readers may stress the literary artfulness of the book, rather than seeking a deeper level of meaning. Instead of teaching a message, the book may simply be entertainment; Jonah's foibles may be intended to invite laughter, rather than to foster learning or reflection.[13]

Other readers focus on the ending of the book without ascertaining a clear meaning in either God's words or Jonah's silence. For these interpreters, Jonah is not a book with a message so much as it is a riddle—and, perhaps, a riddle without an answer. God's perplexing question invites us to offer our own answers without signaling which, if any, answer is correct. Inscrutability may even be a sign of divine power, as some Christian and Jewish theological arguments have held. Or the Book of Jonah may be a proto-postmodern work, playing with language and meaning but never fixing on a single message.

The Message Depends upon the Textual Layer

Another possibility, and one that we ourselves find attractive, is that the message of Jonah depends upon the diachronic layer of text under consideration. As we describe in chapter 1, the Book of Jonah has a multistage history of composition. The oldest layer of the text consists only of events in Jonah 3 and 4—Jonah's prophesying in Nineveh, Nineveh's fast and repentance, and God's creation and destruction of the plant. No flight toward Tarshish, no pious sailors, no giant fish, and no psalm appear. Some of the more memorable details from Jonah 3—4 are also missing from the original story, including the animals' participation in the fast and Jonah's several vocal expressions that he would be better off dead. In this oldest version of the text, nothing suggests that Jonah is a comic figure or a less-than-serious prophet. Similarly, the fantastic features of the narrative, including the adventure story of chapter 1, are missing. Instead, the story is a fairly standard story of prophecy, one that emphasizes divine power and freedom. Jonah prophesies, the people repent, and God changes his mind about their destruction. God's freedom, including the freedom to change his mind, is central here, especially in this version of the narrative where Jonah never expresses anger about the outcome of the prophecy. Instead, the focus is on divine power. There is the suggestion that God should care about Nineveh (4:10), but the point is made without setting up Jonah as a foil. The story thus functions as a narrative of successful prophecy.

The expansion of the text through the additions to chapters 1, 3, and 4 substantially changes both the character of Jonah and the overall message of the book. Jonah becomes a much more fleshed-out character. It is through textual expansion that he becomes the prophet who flees, suggesting he is a comic (or perhaps righteously disobedient) figure. His internment in the fish can similarly be interpreted as either an interval of torture (a serious reading of the narrative) or a comical interlude well suited for an adventure tale (a comic or pleasure-directed reading). The revision of the text also adds Jonah's several statements in chapter 4 that he wishes to die, suggesting that he is either highly dramatic, extremely angry, or some mixture of the two. In any case, this is a very different representation from the good prophet of the older story. It is the expansion of the Jonah story and the added details about his character that also open the possibility for such binary arguments as the one that sees the Book of Jonah being about universalism (represented by God) over and against particularism (represented by Jonah). This sort of reading only makes sense with the more robust characterization of Jonah represented by the expanded text. Similarly, arguments that Jonah fails to grasp the importance of mercy, forgiveness, or even environmental stewardship often emphasize Jonah's anger and his criticism of YHWH. These details, as important as they may be, only occur in the expanded text, not the original narrative.

Finally, it is worth noting that the psalm in chapter 2 has its own distinct message, focused on thanking God for saving the psalmist's life. While the larger theme of thanksgiving can be integrated, if awkwardly, into the Jonah narrative (Jonah is, after all, saved, though not perhaps as he would like),[14] it does not really match any of the major arguments about the book's significance, meaning, or message. Instead of forcing it into conformity with the other chapters, we suggest an appreciation of the message of the psalm in its own right.[15]

Conclusion

The question of message remains a compelling one. The Book of Jonah may be a few short chapters, but it raises all kinds of interesting ethical dilemmas: universalism versus particularism, mercy opposed to justice, the problem of forgiveness, and the questions of what we owe to our enemies and to the natural world. Indeed, part of the genius of the book is the way it makes all of these lines of inquiry and exploration possible. We may never agree on a single message of the Book of Jonah. Even Jonah himself has no satisfactory answer to God's question. But the very act of inquiry into the text remains a deeply rewarding, and revealing, process of interpretation.

6
The Mysteries of Jonah

Even though it contains a relatively straightforward story, there are certain things about the Book of Jonah that have puzzled and fascinated its readers for centuries. In this chapter we consider four such mysteries of the text that are particularly intriguing, not least of all because they have proven to be difficult to solve and people continue to wrestle with them. They touch on issues related to geography, grammar, logic, and the narrative's plot, and sometimes they escape the notice of even Jonah's most attentive readers. Shining a light on these riddles can help us appreciate how complex and intricate this brief biblical book really is.

Where Was Tarshish?

When Jonah tried to flee God's initial call, where was he headed? In a sense, the answer to that question is obvious because it is stated twice in a single verse (1:3) that Tarshish was his destination. Jonah himself acknowledges this in the book's final chapter when he tells YHWH that he attempted to run away to Tarshish because the deity's merciful and compassionate nature was too much for him to handle (4:2). At the same time, where is Tarshish? Scholars have suggested a number of places for its

48

exact location. That same verse in the opening chapter simply identifies Tarshish twice as "away from the presence of YHWH," but it doesn't provide any information about where it was or even what direction Jonah went as he tried to flee. Given the fact that Joppa, his point of departure, was a port city on the Mediterranean Sea, all we can say with certainty is that the ship he boarded was not sailing east.

Other ancient sources locate Tarshish in various places. The Septuagint identifies it with Carthage in North Africa. The first-century CE Jewish historian Josephus, whose opinion on the issue remains popular to the present day, located Tarshish at Tarsus in Cilicia (modern Turkey). Writers, both ancient and modern, have proposed other candidates for the site of Tarshish that include Crete, Cyprus, Sardinia, India, Arabia, Tartessos in southern Spain, and even Britain. The wide range of possibilities has inspired one scholar to compose a "Top Ten" list of alternatives for Tarshish's location.[1]

Several places have vied for the top spot on that list in recent times. One is Tartessos in the southwestern portion of the Iberian Peninsula at the mouth of the Guadalquivir River. Its great distance from Israel at the other end of the Mediterranean Sea is one reason for its appeal as the site of Tarshish. Another is the presence of metals and other wealth in Tartessos, something that is associated with Tarshish in other biblical passages (Jer 10:9; Ezek 27:12; 38:13). On the other hand, the fact that other places in the western Mediterranean are not mentioned in the Hebrew Bible could be a point against identifying Tartessos with Tarshish.

Among the other locations that have been proposed for Tarshish in recent years, two in particular stand out: Tarsus and an unidentified site on the coast of the Arabian Sea or the Indian Ocean. Tarsus, the hometown of the New Testament author Paul, is in the eastern Mediterranean near Israel. Several aspects of it align well with how Tarshish is described in the Bible, including its engagement in international trade, its close relations with Phoenicia, and its probable status as the capital of a kingdom.[2] A possible drawback to this explanation is that, given the location of Jonah's hometown of Gath-Hepher (according to 2 Kgs 14:25), it would have made more sense for him to leave from the ports of Akko or Tyre rather than Joppa if he were looking for a ship bound for Tarsus.

Julia Montenegro and Arcadio del Castillo have proposed an unidentified location on either the Arabian Sea or the Indian Ocean as the most likely site for Tarshish.[3] They base their suggestion on biblical passages that mention trading expeditions involving Tarshish that imply a location southeast of Israel rather than in the Mediterranean. Those passages link Tarshish with Ophir, which has been variously located in Arabia, Ethiopia, or India and would have involved travel on the Red Sea or the Indian Ocean rather than the Mediterranean. In addition, lists of some of the goods traded with Tarshish mention items like ivory, monkeys, and peacocks that would not have been present in the Mediterranean. Montenegro and del Castillo conclude that Jonah would have fled south or southeast rather than west, and that is why he chose to leave from the port of Joppa.

John Day has effectively challenged the theory that Tarsus should be identified with Tarshish, and the evidence he garners also raises questions about the Arabian/Indian location put forward by Montenegro and de Castillo.[4] His argument begins by noting that in Psalm 72:10 Sheba (Yemen) and Seba (east Africa) are juxtaposed with Tarshish as the farthest points in the known world. This works for Tartessos as the westernmost end of the Mediterranean but not for Tarsus, and it shows how when Jonah leaves Joppa for Tarshish he is heading to the extreme other end of the world. Day also addresses certain philological issues related to the place names that demonstrate that Tartessos is a much better fit for Tarshish than Tarsus is. Evidence from other biblical passages supports Day's argument. First, Ezekiel 27:12–24 and Isaiah 66:19 both list place names that, in each passage, are found in a west-to-east sequence with Tarshish in the first position, indicating it is the one farthest to the west. Second, archaeological excavations at Tartessos have uncovered evidence of a sophisticated mining industry that included maritime transport of metals that matches very well the descriptions of Tarshish in Jeremiah 10:9 and Ezekiel 27:12.

It may be that the author of Jonah had the prophet attempt to flee to Tarshish because it functioned as a Shangri-la for the story's readers, an exotic and faraway place meant to evoke mystery and the unknown. Day has helped to clear up some of the mystery for modern readers with his compelling case for Tartessos as the destination Jonah had his sights set on. Less mysterious is why he chose to set sail there in the first place; he was desperate to evade God's call to go to Nineveh, and Tarshish was as far as he could flee in the opposite direction.

Was Jonah's Fish Male or Female?

As well-known as Jonah and his fishy friend are, one aspect of Jonah's fish escapes the attention of most of us. An intriguing grammatical anomaly of the book is the fact that the fish that swallows the prophet changes gender twice. This is impossible to notice in an English translation of the Bible but is obvious in the original text because Hebrew is a language in which every noun is grammatically masculine or feminine.

In 1:17, where the fish swallows Jonah, the Hebrew word that describes it is grammatically masculine (*dāg*), but in the next verse (2:1), as Jonah begins to pray to YHWH, the term switches to its feminine form (*dāgâ*).[5] Then, at the end of the chapter, after Jonah has concluded his prayer, the fish that vomits him out onto dry land is again described as being masculine (2:10). Note that we have avoided using the term "whale," which is the way most people identify the fish. The Hebrew term *dāg* simply refers to a fish or fish-like aquatic creature without specifying its type. The traditional identification of the fish as a whale is understandable in light of its size, but this downplays its likely mythological background since the story of Jonah was probably based on ancient Greek tales about imaginary sea monsters.[6]

The switches in the fish's gender have been explained in various ways. An early and creative attempt was made in *Midrash Yonah*, a rabbinic commentary on the Book of Jonah from the tenth century. According to its account of Jonah's sojourn in the fish, the prophet was quite comfortable for the first three days and did not feel the need to pray. YHWH then came up with a plan to transfer Jonah from this first fish, which was male, to another female fish that was pregnant with 365,000 small fish. The second fish swallowed Jonah immediately after the first one vomited him out, and he began to pray that he be rescued from his uncomfortable new surroundings. This explains the change in the fish's gender from male to female but does not account for the fish's reversion to male in 2:10.[7] Later Jewish commentators like Kimhi (d. 1235) and Rashi (d. 1105) drew upon this tradition in the *Midrash Yonah* to help make sense of the change in the fish's gender.

Since the shift from masculine to feminine requires only the addition of a single letter in Hebrew, some have proposed that the feminine form is due to a scribal error. Such mistakes are well documented in the biblical literature. Grammar handbooks have analyzed the feminine term as an example of the use of a *nomen unitatis* in which the feminine form of a noun, which can sometimes function as a collective, is used to refer to an individual within the group. Jack Sasson maintains that the masculine and feminine forms should be seen as interchangeable because the gender of the fish is irrelevant to the story, and he cites evidence from Akkadian sources to support this view. Kevin Youngblood sees the switch in gender as being intentional as a way of signaling that the now-feminine fish has become a symbol of rebirth and new life for the prophet. Finally, Lena-Sofia Tiemeyer has suggested that what is usually considered to be a feminine form of the noun actually preserves an archaic lengthened noun from older Hebrew that is a pausal form meant to signal the end of a clause.[8] This proposal is supported by the fact that "fish" is the final word in 2:1 in the Hebrew text.

We will probably never know with certainty why the term for Jonah's fish changes gender, but the grammatical inconsistency might provide a clue to the complex composition history of this brief biblical book. As discussed in chapter 4, many scholars consider the psalm-prayer that Jonah utters while in the fish to be a later addition to the book. According to our reconstruction of the book's development (see chapter 1), the two verses that describe the fish as masculine originally came one right after the other as Jonah was first swallowed by the fish and then vomited out (1:17; 2:10). At a later point the poem was inserted, and the person responsible for that addition introduced it by adding the verse that describes the fish as feminine. The editor could have made that change for one of the reasons listed above or for some other reason entirely. Regardless of the motivation, the discrepancy over the gender of Jonah's fish is a grammatical complication that likely points to the complicated history of the development of his story.

How to Interpret Jonah 4:5?

No verse has caused more problems for interpreters of Jonah than 4:5: "Then Jonah went out of the city and sat down east of the city and made a booth for himself there. He sat under it in the shade, waiting to see what would become of the city." This verse has caused controversy for several reasons. (1) It assumes that after Jonah delivered his message to the Ninevites, he remained in the city as the people repented and the king delivered his proclamation (3:5–9), and he was still there when God decided to spare Nineveh (3:10) and while he argued with YHWH (4:1–4). (2) Because Jonah was waiting to see what would happen to the city (or perhaps waiting to see if God's decision would be enacted), the verse also assumes that God had not decided what to do with Nineveh, but YHWH's decision is given in 3:10 and is the reason why the prophet is so unhappy in 4:1–4. (3) The booth that Jonah builds makes the cover that the plant provides in 4:6 unnecessary, but the plant is at the heart of the lesson that ends the book (4:10–11). The issues that 4:5 raises are significant, and the verse has been hotly debated by scholars. Here we offer a brief overview of some of the ways they have been addressed.

A fair number of commentators in recent times have tended to dismiss the problems present in the verse by either ignoring them or downplaying them. Those who do acknowledge them either despair over the lack of a simple solution or claim that the verse has no significant bearing on how the story plays out.[9] Such whitewashing does not pay sufficient attention to the critical role that 4:5 plays in the book's plot development since it describes the point at which Jonah discovers and responds to YHWH's decision regarding Nineveh, which was the entire purpose of the prophet's mission to the city.

The simplest way that some have tried to deal with the problems that 4:5 presents—a solution that can be traced back to the medieval period—is to propose that Jonah realized that the Ninevites' repentance would not be permanent and so he expected that God would change his mind and punish them. This provides a reason for why Jonah waited outside the city, but it does not explain why he waited so long before he left Nineveh. Another proposal that goes back centuries and has been adopted by some modern commentators posits that the bush was necessary to provide shade because the booth Jonah built was insufficient to give him the cover he needed. These are both clever attempts to address some of the problems, but they rely on certain assumptions about Jonah's state of mind and differences between the plant and the booth that are not explicitly mentioned in the text.

Other commentators have engaged in more complex analyses in efforts to smooth out the problems in 4:5, and some of these have entailed deletions or other alterations of the text. Many such changes were originally proposed by German-speaking biblical scholars in the early part of the twentieth century. For example,

Bernhard Duhm proposed deleting the words "and (Jonah) made a booth for himself there. He sat under it in the shade," while his contemporary Julius Wellhausen suggested that only the phrase "in the shade" be removed. A more extreme emendation can be seen in the idea that 4:5 should be returned to its original placement right after 3:4 so that Jonah leaves Nineveh immediately after delivering his message. Each of these proposals would partially address the three problems related to 4:5 mentioned above, but none of them fully resolves all the issues they present.

A final way of interpreting 4:5 that has become popular in recent times but also traces its roots to the medieval period views Jonah's departure from the city as an example of the narrative technique of "flashback" or "forking."[10] In this reading, after Jonah delivers his message, the story describes the people's reception of it and how God spares them (3:5—4:4). Only then does it return to recount how Jonah left Nineveh right after the message was delivered. This requires the first verb in 4:5 to be rendered in the pluperfect tense, and this is precisely how some English versions translate it: "Jonah had gone out of the city...." This makes Jonah's time in Nineveh briefer and helps to resolve the chronological problem, but there are some shortcomings. While the pluperfect tense is well attested in biblical Hebrew, it may not be present in this verse. In addition, quite a bit of narrative action takes place between 3:5 and 4:4, where the flashback occurs, as four scenes featuring different sets of characters are recounted: the Ninevites' repentance (3:5), the king's announcement (3:6–9), God's response to the Ninevites' repentance (3:10), and the exchange between Jonah and God (4:1–4). Such a long delay in a flashback is rare and might suggest that the forking theory should be rejected.

In light of the limitations of the alternatives we've explored here, a solution is unlikely to become apparent in the near future. The mystery of Jonah 4:5 remains unsolved.

Why Does the Book End with a Question?

The Book of Jonah has perhaps the most unusual and, in the view of some, most unsatisfying ending of all the works in the Bible. The final chapter describes a series of strange events, as Jonah expresses to YHWH his displeasure over the fact that Nineveh has not been destroyed, and Jonah builds a booth to give himself shade. God then provides a bush to give him additional cover but also sends a worm that attacks the plant and causes it to wither. Throughout this part of the story Jonah states three times that he wishes he were dead, and the book concludes with the third of three questions YHWH poses to the prophet (4:10–11; AT):

> YHWH said, "You cared about the plant which you did not cultivate or grow, which came about in a night and died in a night. So I should care about Nineveh, shouldn't I—that great city, in which there are more than 120,000 people who don't know their right from their left, not to mention many animals?"

Nahum, another work in the Book of the Twelve, is the only other biblical book that ends with a question, but that one serves a different purpose.[11] Entirely in the form of an oracle that ironically is against Nineveh, the Book of Nahum predicts how the city will be destroyed for its evil ways. The final verse addresses the city with a rhetorical question that implies the Ninevites are getting what they deserve: "For who has ever escaped your endless cruelty?" (Nah 3:19b). The question that concludes Jonah leaves the reader hanging in a way that the one in Nahum doesn't because the former occurs in the middle of a conversation between YHWH and the prophet that abruptly comes to an end. As a result, the point of the book's ending is not completely clear, and various ideas have been put forward as to its purpose.

As noted in our chapter on that topic, the ending of Jonah is closely tied to the question of the book's message (see chapter

5). From that discussion, here we would recall that the final question has been cited in support of diverse suggestions regarding Jonah's message, including God's universal mercy, divine power and authority, the need for an inclusivist mindset rather than an exclusivist one, and the importance of care for and responsibility toward the environment. Some other proposals are less directly connected to the message of the book, and three of them are worth mentioning.

A Prelude to Nahum

As noted above, the Book of Nahum contains an oracle that anticipates (or perhaps describes) the fall of Nineveh in 612 BCE, and it is common, particularly within Judaism, to see a response to Jonah's final question in Nahum. The first section of Nahum makes it clear that the Assyrian capital city will be punished, and reading Jonah in light of the message of Nahum suggests that YHWH's mercy was limited in duration, and Nineveh experienced only a temporary reprieve before it was destroyed. In this way, Nahum, which follows immediately after Jonah in the Greek order of the canon, provides an answer to the question posed at the end of Jonah.

A Parody or Satire

The final section of the book can also be interpreted as a satire or parody meant to belittle either Jonah or perhaps the prophetic office as a whole. After attempting to flee his call, Jonah engages in a halfhearted attempt to deliver YHWH's word to the city, but all its inhabitants, in addition to their animals, nonetheless believe his message. Despite that tremendous success, Jonah pouts and asks God for death. In this reading, YHWH's final question highlights the absurdity of Jonah's actions and is meant to humiliate him and his fellow prophets.[12]

A Swing and a Miss

It is also possible that the Book of Jonah is simply the victim of a bad ending. The author attempted to pull everything together and close with a flourish but couldn't quite succeed, or at least that's how some people view it today. Of course, it might be that the ending was less ambiguous for its original readers, and we respond to it the way we do because of the cultural and chrono-logical distance that exists between us and them.

Clearly, the ending of Jonah and the question it contains has generated its own set of questions about the book's meaning and message. The variety of responses to those questions suggests that there is no single solution to the ending's mystery, and perhaps that's the whole point. Maybe it's the best way to wrap up a strange tale about an ambivalent figure who was more successful than any other prophet in the history of Israel and was miserable as a result. Jonah's final unanswered question has become our own.

Further Interpretive Riddles

In this chapter we have focused on four questions that have loomed large for scholars in their attempts to understand the Book of Jonah, but other puzzles emerge from a careful reading of the story. Three others have piqued our curiosity and have led to some interesting and entertaining conversations among us even if some have been unaddressed in scholarship. We'll mention them in the order in which they arise in the story and offer some thoughts on how we've tried to unravel them.[13]

Why Didn't Jonah Jump Overboard?

Jonah's attempt to flee is quashed by the storm that YHWH sends to prevent the ship from making its journey to Tarshish. When the sailors ask him what they should do, Jonah acknowl-edges that he is the one responsible for the tempest and tells them that it will stop if they toss him into the sea. Instead of heeding his advice, the crew opt for the dangerous maneuver of attempting to return to land. Only when this proves unsuccessful do they throw the prophet into the water (1:11–15). If he was so sure that he was the cause of their distress, why didn't Jonah just jump overboard? We believe that the reason he doesn't take the initiative is likely due to the book's connection to ancient Greek literature that was mentioned earlier in this chapter. In Hellenistic seafaring tales and legends, the hero is sometimes assaulted, robbed, and thrown into the drink by the crew, and so this aspect of the biblical story probably betrays its Greek roots.

Where and What Did Jonah Prophesy?

Jonah eventually makes it to Nineveh, which is described as a city that it took three days to walk through (3:3). According to the story, after entering it he had hardly walked one day when he proclaimed his message, but there is no indication of where Jonah was when he delivered it. We see this as an example of the exaggeration and hyperbole that characterize the story because the archaeological evidence indicates that the city of Nineveh was nowhere near as large as the book describes it to be. A later editor was responsible for adding these hyperbolic elements, and we think the original story had Jonah deliver his message as soon as he entered Nineveh at the city gate. A city's gate served as its hub of commerce and social interaction in antiquity.

Additionally, the story neglects to describe precisely what Jonah said or meant to say when he spoke to the Ninevites. Most translations render his words as "Forty days more and Nineveh is overturned" or something similar. But the last word translates a Hebrew term that can mean either "destroyed" or "transformed," which can refer to a behavioral or inner change. Was Jonah referring to the destruction of the city or the transformation and conversion of its inhabitants that comes to pass in the story? We think it likely that the author/editor had Jonah use an ambiguous word to hedge his bets. Whatever the outcome, Jonah had "predicted" it.

Why Was the King Late?

Upon hearing Jonah's message, the people of Nineveh immediately take it to heart and begin to mend their ways by proclaiming a fast and donning sackcloth, two traditional signs of repentance (3:5). After this, the king issues a proclamation that orders his subjects to fast and put on sackcloth. Why would he command them to do the very things they have already done? In our view, this inconsistency is further evidence of the development of the story over time. In the Septuagint's Greek translation, the verb forms suggest that the king's decree in 3:6–8a was added to an older report about the people's repentance. This might have been done to ridicule the king for lagging behind, or perhaps it's meant to be a statement about the ineptitude and pomposity of rulers.

Conclusion

It is perhaps fitting that Jonah, one of only two biblical books that end with a question, has itself been the subject of so many unanswered questions. On its surface the story appears straightforward, but the more we dig, the more questions we uncover. This is undoubtedly one reason why the tale has fascinated, amused, and puzzled its readers through the ages. Everyone loves a good mystery, and the Book of Jonah is full of them.

7
The Postbiblical Jonah

This chapter treats an aspect of the biblical literature that is often called its reception history, a term that refers to how the Bible has been cited, used, and interpreted by individuals and groups. The Book of Jonah has enjoyed a rich and varied reception history, and it would not be an exaggeration to say that it has been among the most frequently referenced biblical books throughout history. Limitations of space precluding a full account of the many fascinating ways Jonah has been received, our treatment here can provide only a representative sampling. We begin with an overview of Jonah's reception history within the three monotheistic religions, and then we discuss some examples of the ways Jonah has been featured in literature, music, and art.[1]

Jewish Interpretations of Jonah

The Book of Jonah plays an important role in Jewish religious practice. On the holiday of Yom Kippur (the Day of Atonement), the Book of Jonah is read aloud in the synagogue in its entirety. Because Jonah describes God's compassion toward Nineveh, the book is paired with Micah 7:18–20, which describes God's compassion for Israel. Jonah also figures in the traditional prayer of the High Holy Days (Rosh Hashanah and Yom Kippur), the most holy days in Judaism.[2]

Many traditions of Jewish interpretation surround the Book of Jonah. The earliest postbiblical references come from the Second Temple period (516 BCE–70 CE). Jonah appears in Deuterocanonical books such as 2 Esdras (where he is identified as a "leader" of the people, 2 Esd 1:39) and 3 Maccabees 6:8. In the *Lives of the Prophets*, which dates to the first century CE, a version of Jonah's story appears, and he is identified as the son of the widow of Zarephath that Elijah brings back to life (1 Kgs 17:17–24).[3] Other Jewish texts continue this identification. Jonah also appears in the Jewish historian Josephus's work *Antiquities of the Jews* (Book X, chapter 10, 1–2), which gives a version of the biblical story but omits Nineveh's repentance and the events that follow.

The most lively and intriguing Jewish interpretations of Jonah come from midrash, which is a genre of biblical exegesis or commentary (the word "midrash" comes from the root *drash*, meaning "to expound"). Most midrashim date from the late antique and medieval periods; often, the traditions are older than the texts where they are found. *Pirqe Rabbi Eliezer*, an eighth- or ninth-century CE midrashic text that contains many biblical retellings, has an extensive discussion of Jonah. The text adds many fantastical details. When the fish first meets Jonah, it is in distress because it is about to be eaten by the Leviathan, a primordial sea monster. Jonah flashes his circumcised penis and intimidates the Leviathan, saving the fish. The grateful fish responds by taking Jonah on an undersea tour (a creative interpretation of Jonah 2 and its references to various locations such as the foundations of the earth). How is Jonah able to see these sights? Fortunately, the fish's eyes function as large windows, and a magical pearl provides light. When the fish vomits Jonah out, the sailors see what has happened and are so amazed that they travel to Jerusalem and become circumcised.[4] While *Pirqe Rabbi Eliezer* does not cover the events of Jonah 3 or 4, it offers a rich reimagining of the book's first two chapters.

Other midrashic texts also offer creative expansions on Jonah's story. *Midrash Yonah*, a tenth-century text, is the source for the claim that God originally houses Jonah in a male fish, only to transfer him to a female fish when he becomes too comfortable (see discussion in chapter 6). Unlike *Pirqe Rabbi Eliezer*, this text does include the repentance of the Ninevites—including some speculation over whether this repentance was genuine.[5] It also suggests that the reason Jonah is so angry and unpleasant in chapter 4 is that his clothes were destroyed inside the fish, leaving him exposed to the elements.[6] The same claim is made by multiple other Jewish interpreters, including the influential twelfth-century commentator Abraham ibn Ezra.

Another frequently repeated Jewish claim is that Jonah's great flaw is his passion for Israel, which is even greater than his passion for God. As another midrash, the *Mekhilta de Rabbi Ishmael*, puts it, "Jonah defended the honor of the child [Israel], rather than the honor of the Father [God]."[7] This also explains why Jonah is so reluctant to be a prophet: he does not want Nineveh to repent, because he knows the Ninevites are enemies of the Israelites and will do them harm in the future. Ibn Ezra, for example, also makes this argument. An alternative explanation for Jonah's reluctance offered by the Jewish sources is that he does not want to be a false prophet (as he will become if God changes his mind and spares Nineveh). This tradition occurs, for example, in *Pirqe Rabbi Eliezer*.

A quite different account of Jonah can be found in the Zohar, a text foundational for Kabbalah (Jewish mysticism). The Zohar offers an allegorical reading of Jonah 1—2 in which Jonah represents the soul, the ship represents the body, the captain represents the good inclination, the conversation with the sailors represents the trial of the soul, the sea represents the graveyard, and the fish represents death. Jonah's three days in the fish are the three days in the grave before the soul ascends, leaving the body to rot. The Zohar makes much of the Hebrew verb *yrd*, which means "to go down" and which occurs several times in Jonah 1. The Zohar interprets this to mean the descent of the soul into the physical world.[8] The soul's difficult and tormented journey through the world is a frequent image in medieval Judaism, an older tradition that the Zohar repurposes.[9]

Christian Interpretations of Jonah

Christian interpretation of Jonah begins in the New Testament, with three passages that refer to the "sign of Jonah" (Matt 12:38–41; 16:1–4; Luke 11:29–32). Scholars have different interpretations about what exactly is meant by the "sign of Jonah."[10] The phrase is ambiguous and can be understood in at least three different ways:[11] (1) as a genitive of apposition (the sign, i.e., Jonah himself); (2) as an objective genitive (the sign that Jonah experienced); (3) as a subjective genitive (the sign that Jonah gave to others). This means that the sign could refer to Jonah himself, to his deliverance from the fish, to the sparing of Nineveh, or to the prophecy Jonah spoke to the Ninevites. It is also possible that Matthew and Luke intend different meanings for the "sign of Jonah."[12] Scholars have also perceived other references to Jonah in the New Testament, such as Paul's description of the resurrection "on the third day, in accordance with the scriptures" in 1 Corinthians 15:4.[13]

First Corinthians 15:4 portrays Jonah typologically, as a type of Christ. Such typological reading of Jonah is especially apparent in early Christian art, particularly in the catacombs, where scenes of Jonah's internment in and expulsion from the fish are popular as imagery of resurrection. However, literary references to Jonah are scant among the earliest Christian interpreters until the patristic writers. Figures such as Jerome, Tertullian, and Cyril of Jerusalem, among others, associate Jonah with Jesus Christ, understanding the "sign of Jonah" to allude to Jesus's death and resurrection.[14] We find particular emphasis on Jonah

2, with Jonah's three days in the belly of the fish and his descent to the underworld in the psalm interpreted as types of Christ's time in hell. Thus, Tertullian, among others, argues that the fish's vomiting out of Jonah represents the resurrection.[15] Also, Jonah's prophecy to the Ninevites does not come to them until after the expulsion from the fish, just as Christ's preaching to the Gentiles occurs only after the resurrection.

The writings of Augustine, the most influential early Christian interpreter, attest anti-Jewish or antisemitic tendencies, as he sees Jonah not only as a sign of Jesus but also as personification of Israel and Judaism and thus opposed to the Christian message of God's love for everyone in Christ.[16] This antisemitic interpretation gained new vitality in the early modern period with Martin Luther and has affected Christian interpretation of Jonah up to the present.

Christian interpretations of Jonah shifted dramatically during the Reformation, as the primary image of Jonah as a type of Christ gave way to other representations of Jonah. At the same time, the focus on the fish as a miraculous sign of the resurrection dissipated in favor of other interests and concerns. Two of the most prominent Reformation leaders, Martin Luther and John Calvin, both wrote commentaries on Jonah. Luther authored two of them, one in Latin in 1525 and a more extensive one in German a year later.

As noted above, Luther was influenced by Augustine and perpetuated a similar double reading of Jonah as both the "dove" (the meaning of the name Jonah) symbolizing the Holy Spirit *and* "the Jew," representing Judaism and its failings.[17] This reading, with its antisemitic edge, comes to replace the Jonah-as-Christ understanding and becomes a dominant Christian interpretation of the book. Luther actually rejects the Jonah-as-Christ interpretation along with that of his time in the fish as a type of the resurrection. Rather, he identifies the worm that attacks the plant as a symbol of Christ, based on Psalm 22:6, "I am a worm and no man;" the plant is Judaism, once flourishing but then withered by divine ordinance.[18]

Calvin's commentary on Jonah is concerned mainly with questions of sin and self-discipline; Jonah represents the struggle to follow God. Calvin also identifies divine grace and mercy in the story, both in the word of God coming to Jonah a second time and in the sparing of Nineveh. The differences between Luther's and Calvin's commentaries highlight the fact that there is little agreement among Reformation theologians about how to interpret Jonah.

In modern Christian usage, selections from the Book of Jonah are found in the lectionaries of most denominations for different occasions. Jonah 3 (or parts of it) is the most common source for lectionary readings, followed by chapter 4. For Roman Catholic and Orthodox Christians, selections from Jonah are typically read during Lent. Since Vatican II, Catholics have read Jonah 3 on the Wednesday of the first full week of Lent.

Islamic Interpretations of Jonah

Jonah is revered as a prophet in Islam, and he is the only one of the Bible's major and minor prophets who is mentioned by name in the Qur'an. His story is also found in the writings that make up the corpus of Islamic literature known as the "Stories of the Prophets." Jonah is referred to in a more limited way in the hadith, the set of Muslim traditions that preserves the sayings and writings of the Prophet Muhammad. Here we provide an overview of how Jonah is presented in these Islamic sources.[19]

Jonah is referred to by name five times in the Qur'an, where he is also called "the one of the fish" and "the companion of the fish." Two of those occurrences simply identify him in a list of some of the messengers that God has sent to humanity throughout history. In one passage of the Qur'an, "the one of the fish" tries to flee and assumes God has no authority over him. He then recognizes his mistake and cries out in the darkness, and the

deity responds by saving him from his distress (Q al-Anbiyā'
21:87–88). This is likely an allusion to the biblical scene in which
Jonah utters a prayer while inside the great fish (Jonah 2:1–10).
In another passage referring to that same scene, Jonah remains
unnamed, and Muhammad is reminded to be patient and not be
like the "companion of the fish" who called out when he was
in trouble (Q al-Qalam 68:48–50). Both of these passages lack
narrative details, which is commonly the case in the text of the
Qur'an, and so their connection to the biblical account is minimal.

By contrast, the other qur'anic text related to Jonah contains
some of the elements of the biblical book, including his flight to a
ship, the fish swallowing him, the plant that God causes to grow
over him, and his being sent to a people who repent (Q al-Ṣaffāt
37:139–148). The qur'anic version never names the place where
God sends Jonah, but Islamic tradition identifies it as Nineveh.

In general, Jonah comes across more positively in the
Qur'an than he does in the Bible, where he is a petulant and
angry figure.[20] An important difference between the two is that
the Islamic Jonah, unlike his biblical counterpart, acknowledges
his error and expresses repentance and remorse. Muslims therefore view him as an example to follow and a reminder that God
is always ready to show mercy to those who admit their mistakes
and ask for forgiveness.

Jonah is hardly mentioned in the thousands of hadith traditions that report the words and actions of Muhammad. Most references to him are found in a group of sayings that have the prophet
of Islam caution people against claiming that they are better than
Jonah. This tradition likely functioned as a way to counteract
claims of Jonah's unworthiness as a prophet due to his anger and
unenthusiastic response to God's call that are mentioned in the
Qur'an. In this way, it probably served to bolster Jonah's reputa-
tion and give him the status that Islam teaches is befitting of all
prophets.

The term "Stories of the Prophets" refers to various works
of Muslim literature that recount events in the lives of prominent

figures of the past, most of whom are mentioned in the Bible. One of the most popular collections of the "Stories of the Prophets" is one written by al-Kisa'i (d. thirteenth century CE), and his version of the Jonah story will be the focus of our attention.[21] After a brief description of Jonah's birth and early life, al-Kisa'i recounts how Jonah is commissioned by God to go to Nineveh. After a half-hearted attempt to avoid that call, Jonah is soon on his way with his entire family, but through a series of events they all disappear, and he is on his own. God advises the prophet that he will get them back if he does what he has been told to do.

Jonah then goes to Nineveh and proclaims his message, one that is modeled on the Islamic profession of faith. The city's inhabitants reject him, but Jonah continues to deliver his message for forty days, to no avail. At God's command, he leaves the city and goes out on a high hill to see what will happen. The city is punished with lightning bolts the size of thunderclouds, which causes the king and all his subjects to express their repentance and ask God's forgiveness.

Jonah then sees a ship about to set sail and he boards it. A storm rises and the crew believes the tempest is Jonah's fault, so they cast lots to determine if he is the cause. Just then, a great fish appears and says, "Jonah, I have come from India in search of you." Jonah jumps into the water, and the fish swallows him and takes him first to the Mediterranean Sea and then to a place called the Coral Castle. At God's command, the fish vomits out Jonah, and he stays for forty days under a plant sent by the deity. After being reprimanded by God, Jonah is reunited with the members of his family, and they all return to their people. Jonah lives among them until he dies, exhorting them to do good and to refrain from evil.

Perhaps the biggest difference between the biblical story and the al-Kisa'i account is the introduction of Jonah's family in the latter, which transforms how we view Jonah and his circumstances. This is not the story of a solitary prophet who reluctantly goes out on his own. It is rather the story of someone who loses everything only to get it all back again after he learns an important lesson about the nature of God. In this way, al-Kisa'i's Jonah resembles Job more than his biblical counterpart.

Jonah in Literature

Though short, the Book of Jonah casts a long shadow over literature. Already in the late antique and medieval periods, Jonah's story was retold in a number of poems. The medieval period also yielded multiple literary treatments of Jonah, including the first English-language treatment of Jonah, the alliterative Middle English poem *Patience* that is the work of the "Pearl Poet," (perhaps best known for another alliterative poem, *Sir Gawain and the Green Knight*). Other early modern authors also took up Jonah or parts of his story, including Marie de France, Dante, and Rabelais.[22]

Perhaps the most famous literary treatment of Jonah is Herman Melville's 1851 novel *Moby-Dick; or, The Whale*, which tells the story of the voyage of the whaling ship the *Pequod* and its doomed journey to hunt down Moby-Dick, the famous great white whale that previously devoured the leg of the ship's captain, Ahab. The book is narrated by Ishmael, who joins the crew of the *Pequod* and is, eventually, the voyage's only survivor. Melville's novel is deeply biblical, and the Book of Jonah plays several important roles. Beyond the nautical setting (compare Jonah 1) and various descriptions of the interiors of whales (Jonah 2), the novel includes multiple explicit references to the story, including a chapter called "Jonah Historically Regarded." Perhaps most famously, shortly before setting sail, Ishmael visits a "Whaleman's Chapel" in New Bedford, where he listens as Father Mapple preaches a sermon on Jonah—included in its entirety in the novel. Mapple stresses the importance of obedience to God, along with the "terrors upon terrors" Jonah faces, anticipating much of what is to come aboard the *Pequod*.[23]

Additional seafaring novels also make reference to Jonah. In *Robinson Crusoe*, for example, Daniel Defoe explicitly compares

Crusoe to Jonah.[24] More recently, Tim Winton's 1984 novel *Shallows* retells the story of Jonah, while also exploring whaling, science, and religion.[25] A more lighthearted example is Carlo Collodi's *The Adventures of Pinocchio* (*Le avventure di Pinocchio*), first published in Italian in 1883.[26] Pinocchio, a wooden puppet, is swallowed by a shark (Ital. *pesce-cana*, literally "dogfish") and forced to live inside it.

Some literary treatments focus less on the ship and the fish, emphasizing, instead, how the book might offer a lens to understand other literary and ethical questions. In particular, a significant body of literature uses Jonah to explore twentieth-century history, especially the Second World War and the Holocaust (Shoah). German theologian and member of the resistance Dietrich Bonhoeffer, who was imprisoned and executed for a failed plot to kill Hitler, wrote a poem called "Jonah" emphasizing the prophet's self-sacrifice.[27] Hebrew-language poets Gabriel Preil and Dan Pagis also wrote poems about Jonah in reference to the Second World War and the Holocaust.[28] Most strikingly, Norma Rosen begins her essay "Justice for Jonah, or, a Biblical Bartleby" by writing, "Show me a text that speaks of God's unbounded mercy, and images of the Holocaust appear before my eyes."[29]

Other writers use Jonah to explore questions of identity, without focusing on a particular historical moment. One extensive tradition uses Jonah to explore Jewish identity, ranging from poems by Adrienne Rich and Yiddish poet Kadia Molodowsky to Wolf Mankowitz's humorous 1956 play, *It Should Happen to a Dog*, to Joshua Max Feldman's novel *The Book of Jonah* (2014), in which the world of New York finance stands in as the setting, and Nineveh becomes Las Vegas (the time in the fish is also absent, replaced by a bender and breakdown).[30] Jonah as a symbolic Jew also appears in some texts written by non-Jews, such as Robert Frost's play in verse, "A Masque of Mercy," which imagines a conversation between Paul and Jonah.[31]

Jonah does not always symbolize a Jewish character. In Tony Kushner's Pulitzer Prize–winning play, *Angels in America*,

Prior Walter, a secular gay WASP with AIDS, is commissioned as a prophet and explicitly associated with Jonah.[32] Important works of African American literature also make use of Jonah and his story, most famously Zora Neale Hurston's novel *Jonah's Gourd Vine* (1934), which tells the story of John Pearson, a preacher, philanderer, and Jonah figure.[33] Lucille Clifton's short poem "jonah" imagines the prophet on a slave ship in the Middle Passage.[34] Iranian author Amir Ahmadi Arian, meanwhile, reimagines Jonah in Tehran in 2005 and 2006, early in the presidency of Mahmoud Ahmadinejad. Arian's 2020 novel, *Then the Fish Swallowed Him*, retells Jonah based on both the biblical and the qur'anic account.

Jonah in Music

Numerous discussions of Jonah's reception in music focus on the classical genres,[35] but the book's reception in modern popular music as a whole has not received the same attention.[36] Popular music in which Jonah is received spans different genres—folk, country, rock, hip hop, reggae, and many others, and many of the artists who wrote or performed these songs are top sellers, even household names, including figures like Elvis Presley, Paul Simon, and Elton John. In popular music, Jonah is in a class with major heroes of the Bible like Moses, Elijah, and Jesus.

Jonah is best known in popular music for his encounter with the fish or "whale." Some songs are explicitly religious. An example is "Jonah and the Whale" on Louis Armstrong's *Louis and the Good Book* album, which recounted the biblical story with a few liberties.[37] Country songs by Hank Snow, Kitty Wells, and Roger Miller in the 1950s and early 1960s exhibit the same religious interest.[38] Lena Horne's "If You Believe" and Gold City's "I Believe" even cite belief in the historicity of the Jonah story as an article of faith necessary for salvation.[39] Although they do not say so, the episode with the fish is almost certainly the one that the songs have in mind as a test of belief. The spiritual "Didn't

My Lord Deliver Daniel" cites Jonah's release from the whale as deliverance from slavery and oppression.[40]

A few songs that are religious in nature highlight other portions of the Jonah story besides the fish episode. Jonah was a favorite of Vengeance Rising, a groundbreaking Christian metal band in the late 1980s and early 1990s, whose interpretations resembled the allegory of Church fathers. Its song "Out of the Will" saw the "gnarly storm" in Jonah as a warning of the consequences of disobedience and Jonah's rescue as a type of Christ's resurrection. "Fill This Place with Blood" compared Nineveh with the thief on the cross as examples of second chances available because of Christ's shedding of blood. Then, "Counting Corpses" mentioned Assyria's fall long after its reprieve in Jonah as divine wrath against nonbelievers.[41]

Some songs focus on Jonah for musical, rather than religious, reasons, perhaps because of the psalm in Jonah 2. Jonah is included in the celebration of music and singing of Elvis Presley's "Sing Children Sing."[42] Paul Simon ("Jonah") likewise asserts that it was not a whale that swallowed Jonah but a song.[43] The hip hop artist Bow Wow refers to singing hymns like Jonah.[44]

Alongside the religious and musical interests is a longstanding tradition of nonreligious and even playful interpretations of Jonah. The braggadocious folk song "I Was Born About 10,000 Years Ago" in one version attributes the whale's release of Jonah to his garlicky breath.[45] "The Preacher and the Bear" tells of a preacher who skipped church on Sunday to go hunting and was treed by a bear.[46] The preacher prayed to be rescued like Jonah and begged that God at least not help the bear. "It Ain't Necessarily So" from the 1935 musical *Porgy and Bess* questioned the Bible's claim that Jonah lived in a whale for three days.[47]

Jonah appears as part of a nautical theme in popular music and is often conflated with Noah. Depeche Mode cast Jonah as a whaler.[48] The Israeli band Orphaned Land released an album in 2004 entitled *Mabool*, meaning "flood," that includes a song ("The Storm Still Rages Inside") about Jonah.[49] Elton John and

Leon Russell's "Hey Ahab" (2010) combines Jonah with Captain Ahab from *Moby-Dick*.[50]

Some songs mine Jonah for social and political causes. In Skyclad's "Terminus" (1991) Jonah witnesses environmental damage in the oceans, and their album *Jonah's Ark* playfully combines the two best known biblical characters who deal with waters—Noah and Jonah. The album also includes the song "It Wasn't Meant to End This Way" with death piloting Jonah's ark, foreboding the fate of the oceans.[51] Reggae artists Buju Banton and Luciano commend Jonah for trusting in God and imply that if he were alive today, he would also trust God to find a solution to gun violence and to summon youth to appreciate their religious and cultural traditions.[52]

The most frequent use of the Jonah story in popular music expresses personal feelings of isolation and abandonment but also of freedom and joy. "Cuckoo Cocoon" by Genesis and "Hallelujah" by rapper T.I., both compare jail time to Jonah's stay in the fish.[53] "The Whale Has Swallowed Me" and Guster's "Jonah" voice the sense of isolation and entrapment felt by Jonah.[54] Conversely, Jonah's release is grounds for optimism in "Ac-Cen-Tchu-Ate the Positive" by Harold Arlen and Johnny Mercer.[55] Jonah's experience of being tossed about, swallowed, and released is a symbol for romantic relationships in the two songs titled "Jonah" by Breathe and Wussy.[56]

As this brief survey shows, fascination with Jonah in popular music has been constant and shows no indication of abating in the future.

Jonah in Art

Jonah has been a popular subject in artwork, and three scenes from his story have been depicted frequently: (1) the sailors tossing him overboard; (2) his being swallowed by or his exit from the fish; and (3) Jonah reclining under the plant that God sent to provide him shade. Here we will discuss some examples of how Jonah's encounter with the fish has been represented in the three monotheistic religious traditions, and then consider a number of other attempts to capture that episode through the medium of painting.

Archaeological excavations recently undertaken at Huqoq in northern Israel have uncovered a fifth-century CE synagogue that contains an interesting mosaic of Jonah as he is being swallowed by the fish. It is a highly unusual scene because the fish swallowing Jonah is being swallowed by another fish that is itself being swallowed by a third fish. Only the prophet's legs are visible as they protrude out of the fish's mouth. It might be that this depiction is meant to reflect the grammatical anomaly that in the Hebrew text the fish switches from male to female and back to male (see chapter 6). Alternatively, the mosaic might be an indication of familiarity with certain rabbinic interpretations of the story in which Jonah relocates from one fish to another. Regardless of how the scene is understood, it provides a humorous portrayal of what happened after the prophet was thrown from the boat.[57]

Jonah was a popular subject in Christian funerary art during the first few centuries CE probably because aspects of his story, particularly his survival within the fish, became associated with the themes of death and resurrection. This is best seen in an exquisite stone sarcophagus from the late third century, currently in the Vatican Museum, on which the scenes of Jonah being swallowed and expelled are the focus of attention. In these scenes and several others on the sarcophagus, water figures prominently, and this is likely due to the common Christian understanding of baptism as a symbol of death and resurrection.[58]

Representation of the human form in art is less common in Islam than it is in Judaism and Christianity, but Jonah occasionally appears in works by Muslims. An example can be seen in a Persian painting by an unknown artist from the early fifteenth century that shows Jonah emerging from the mouth of the fish. He is being deposited back on dry land underneath the plant provided by God that is meant to give him shade, as mentioned in both the Bible and the Qur'an. An angelic being, perhaps Gabriel, hovers above the fish and offers a garment to the naked prophet as a way of expressing the Muslim belief that God takes care of and provides for those who are chosen to deliver the divine message.[59]

Jonah's experience with the fish is the scene depicted most frequently by painters. This can be seen, for example, in a work by Tintoretto titled "Jonah Leaves the Whale's Belly" (1577–78) in which the prophet appears to emerge from the fish while sitting on its massive tongue and wearing only a loincloth. As he exits, Jonah is confronted by another figure who is gesticulating and speaking to him in an animated fashion, presumably meant to capture the moment when God repeats the command to go to Nineveh.[60] Some three centuries later, the French artist James Jacques Joseph Tissot painted his "Jonah the Prophet" (ca. 1888) as part of a series of works on biblical prophets. As a wave crashes on the shore behind him, a distressed Jonah is back on dry land and the only evidence of the cause of his trauma is a tailfin about to disappear beneath the water's surface.[61] A more terrifying presentation of the prophet and his predicament is found in "Jonah" (ca. 1885) by the American painter Albert Pinkham Ryder. As Jonah flails about in the raging sea while the ship he has just been tossed from surfs down a mountain of water, God serenely looks on from above and blesses the chaotic scene.[62] More whimsical is Salvador Dali's "Jonah and the Whale" (1975), a work that captures the moment just before the prophet is swallowed by the fish, which takes the shape of a wave that is about to engulf a surfer who is attempting to ride it.[63]

The artistic fascination with Jonah and his fish has continued into the twenty-first century. The Hawaiian artist Dennis McGeary's "Jonah" (2001) offers an abstract vision evoking the storm, the ship, and the fish; the vision is bookended by two images of the prophet, one as he descends into the depths and the other as he ponders his fate after being swallowed.[64] Finally, Debbie Turner Chaver's 2005 watercolor painting "Jonah Gone

Fishing" shows the faceless prophet coming out of the open mouth of a very large fish. He is holding a staff in the shape of a cross, and he is entwined in seaweed that also dangles from the staff.[65]

Conclusion

The works discussed here are a very small sample of the many ways that artists have drawn upon and depicted the story of Jonah. His encounter with the fish has held special appeal for them throughout the ages both because of its rich symbolism and its unusual nature. Jewish, Christian, and Muslim artists have turned to the story to convey and affirm beliefs that are central to their religious traditions, and artists from all perspectives have used their skills to provide new interpretations of an old tale about a man and a fish.

Notes

Chapter 1

1. This reconstruction of the composition of Jonah has previously appeared in Steven L. McKenzie, Rhiannon Graybill, and John Kaltner, "Underwater Archaeology: The Compositional Layers of the Book of Jonah," *VT* 70, no. 1 (2020): 83–103; and Rhiannon Graybill, John Kaltner, and Steven L. McKenzie, *Jonah: A New Translation with Commentary*, AYB 24H (New Haven/London: Yale University Press, 2023). We discuss the reconstruction in greater detail in those publications.

2. The NRSV obscures the correspondence by translating the two verbs in v. 2 as "Go at once" and the same verb (arise) in v. 3 as "set out." Its translation of 3:2–3 is better for showcasing the correspondence: "'Get up, go to Nineveh, that great city, and proclaim to it the message that I tell you.' So Jonah set out and went to Nineveh, according to the word of the Lord. Now Nineveh was an exceedingly large city, a three days' walk across."

3. Herodotus, *Hist.* 1.23.

4. On this and other superlatives, see D. Winton Thomas, "A Consideration of Some Unusual Ways of Expressing the Superlative in Hebrew," *VT* 3 (1950): 209–24, esp. 211, 216. Some commentators argue for a more literal understanding: "to God." But the superlative is supported by the context between "great" and "three days' walk," both focused on size.

Chapter 2

1. His views on the literary relationships within the Book of the Twelve are laid out in James D. Nogalski, *Redactional Processes in the Book of the Twelve*, BZAW 218 (Berlin/New York: De Gruyter, 1993). See also James D. Nogalski, *The Book of the Twelve: Hosea–Jonah*, SHBC (Macon, GA: Smyth & Helwys, 2011), 3–4.

2. See Marvin A. Sweeney, "Sequence and Interpretation in the Book of the Twelve," in *Reading and Hearing the Book of the Twelve*, ed. James D. Nogalski and Marvin A. Sweeney, SymS 15 (Atlanta: Society of Biblical Literature, 2000), 49–64; and Marvin A. Sweeney, "Synchronic and Diachronic Concerns in Reading the Book of the Twelve Prophets," in *Perspectives on the Formation of the Book of the Twelve*, ed. Rainer Albertz, James D. Nogalski, and Jakob Wöhrle, BZAW 433 (Berlin/New York: De Gruyter, 2012), 25–30.

3. For a discussion of issues related to the Book of the Twelve in the Dead Sea Scrolls, see Mika S. Pajunen and Hanne von Weissenberg, "The Book of Malachi, Manuscript 4Q76 (4QXII[a]), and the Formation of the 'Book of the Twelve,'" *JBL* 134 (2015): 731–51.

4. Ehud Ben Zvi, "Twelve Prophetic Books or 'The Twelve': A Few Preliminary Considerations," in *Forming Prophetic Literature: Essays on Isaiah and the Twelve in Honor of John D. W. Watts*, ed. James W. Watts and Paul R. House, JSOTSup 235 (Sheffield: Sheffield Academic Press, 1996), 125–56.

5. Diana V. Edelman, "Jonah among the Twelve in the MT: The Triumph of Torah over Prophecy," in *The Production of Prophecy: Constructing Prophecy and Prophets in Yehud*, ed. Diana V. Edelman and Ehud Ben Zvi (London/New York: Routledge, 2014), 161.

6. A fuller discussion of the genre of the Book of Jonah is found in chapter 3. See Aaron Schart, "The Jonah-Narrative within the Book of the Twelve," in *Perspectives on the Formation of the Book of the Twelve*, ed. Rainer Albertz, James D. Nogalski, and Jakob Wöhrle, BZAW 433 (Berlin/New York: De Gruyter, 2012), 109–28.

7. His analysis of Jonah can be found in Jakob Wöhrle, "A Prophetic Reflection on Divine Forgiveness: The Integration of the Book of Jonah into the Book of the Twelve," *JHebS* 9 (2009).

8. For these critiques of Wöhrle's work, see Schart, "The Jonah-

Narrative," 120–21; and Klass Spronk, "Jonah, Nahum, and the Book of the Twelve: A Response to Jakob Wöhrle," *JHebS* 9 (2009).

9. See Edelman, "Jonah among the Twelve in the MT," 162; and Ehud Ben Zvi, *Signs of Jonah: Reading and Rereading in Ancient Yehud*, JSOTSup 367 (London: Sheffield Academic Press/Continuum, 2003): 100–115.

Chapter 3

1. John A. Miles, "Laughing at the Bible: Jonah as Parody," *JQR* 65, no. 3 (1975): 168–81; David Marcus, *From Balaam to Jonah: Anti-prophetic Satire in the Hebrew Bible* (Atlanta: Scholars Press, 1995), 145–47; Raymond F. Person, *In Conversation with Jonah: Conversation Analysis, Literary Criticism, and the Book of Jonah*, JSOTSup 220 (Sheffield: Sheffield Academic Press, 1996).

2. M. H. Abrams, *A Glossary of Literary Terms* (New York: Holt, Rinehart & Winston, 1981), 167–68; see also Person, *In Conversation with Jonah*, 84.

3. Marcus, *From Balaam to Jonah*, 10–27; Zev Garber and Bruce Zuckerman, "The Odd Prophet Out and In," in *Lema'an Ziony: Essays in Honor of Ziony Zevit*, ed. Frederick E. Greenspahn and Gary A. Rendsburg (Eugene, OR: Cascade, 2017), 198.

4. Marcus, *From Balaam to Jonah*, 170.

5. Miles, "Laughing at the Bible," 174–75.

6. Arnold J. Band, "Swallowing Jonah: The Eclipse of Parody," *Prooftexts* 10, no. 2 (1990): 177–95.

7. Unfortunately, this argument sometimes takes an antisemitic turn, with Jonah being represented as a stereotype of the small-minded Jew. See further Yvonne Sherwood, *A Biblical Text and Its Afterlives: The Survival of Jonah in Western Culture*, 1st ed. (Cambridge: Cambridge University Press, 2000), 21–32.

8. André LaCocque and Pierre-Emmanuel Lacocque, *Jonah: A Psycho-Religious Approach to the Prophet* (Columbia: University of South Carolina Press, 1990); repr. of *The Jonah Complex* (Atlanta: John Knox, 1981). While Menippean satire takes its name from the Greek cynic Menippus, who lived in the third century BCE, it is most closely associated with the Russian literary critic Mikhail Bakhtin, who offered

an extensive discussion of Menippean satire in his book *Problems of Dostoevsky's Poetics*. Menippean satire is nonhistorical; it mixes literary symbolism and realism and brings different genres together (e.g., poetry and prose, as in Jonah); its characters are often oxymorons (such as the pious foreigners in Jonah or the atypical prophet).

9.   In Matt 12:38–42, Jesus explicitly links the "sign of Jonah" with his time in the tomb.

10.   Julius A. Bewer, *A Critical and Exegetical Commentary on Jonah*, ICC (Edinburgh: T&T Clark, 1912), 4.

11.   Phyllis L. Trible, "Studies in the Book of Jonah" (Columbia University, 1963), Unpublished PhD Dissertation. Trible subsequently published *Rhetorical Criticism: Context, Method, and the Book of Jonah*, Guides to Biblical Scholarship (Minneapolis, MN: Fortress Press, 1994).

12.   James Nogalski, *The Book of the Twelve: Hosea–Jonah*, Smyth & Helwys Bible Commentary (Macon, GA: Smyth & Helwys, 2011), 403, sidebar "The Genre of Jonah."

13.   Alexander Rofé, "Classes in the Prophetical Stories: Didactic Legend and Parable," in *Congress Volume*, ed. J. A. Emerton, VTSup 26 (Leiden: Brill, 1974), 152–70; George M. Landes, "Jonah: A *Māšāl*?," in *Israelite Wisdom: Theological and Literary Essays in Honor of Samuel Terrien*, ed. Samuel L. Terrien and John G. Gammie (Missoula, MT: Scholars Press for Union Theological Seminary, 1978), 148–49. Landes translates *mashal* as "example story."

14.   Janet Howe Gaines, *Forgiveness in a Wounded World: Jonah's Dilemma* (Atlanta: Society of Biblical Literature, 2003).

15.   Jack M. Sasson, *Jonah*, AYB 24B (New York: Doubleday, 1990), 335.

16.   Thomas M. Bolin, *Freedom beyond Forgiveness: The Book of Jonah Re-Examined*, JSOTSup 236 (Sheffield: Sheffield Academic Press, 1997), 48–49.

17.   Judson Mather, "The Comic Art of the Book of Jonah," *Soundings: An Interdisciplinary Journal* 65, no. 3 (1982): 280–91.

18.   Terry Eagleton, "J. L. Austin and the Book of Jonah," *New Blackfriars* 69, no. 815 (1988): 64.

19.   Roger Syren, "The Book of Jonah—a Reversed Diasporanovella?" *SEÅ* 58 (1993): 7–14.

20.   Herman Melville, *Moby-Dick*, ed. Hershel Parker and Harrison

Hayford, 2nd ed., Norton Critical Edition (New York: Norton, 2002 [1851]), 49.

21. Ehud Ben Zvi, *Signs of Jonah: Reading and Rereading in Ancient Yehud*, JSOTSup 267 (London: Sheffield Academic Press/Continuum, 2003), 85; italics original.

22. Gaines, *Jonah's Dilemma*, 24; Barbara Green, *Jonah's Journeys*, Interfaces (Collegeville, MN: Liturgical Press, 2005), 89–91.

Chapter 4

1. See Jonathan Magonet, *Form and Meaning: Studies in Literary Techniques in the Book of Jonah* (Bern: Herbert Lang, 1976), 44–49; Jack M. Sasson, *Jonah*, AYB 24B (New Haven/London: Yale, 1990), 173–201, for parallels in Psalms. Jonathan Kaplan argues that Jonah's psalm is a pastiche of citations but that this was a deliberate strategy by the author of the Book of Jonah; see Kaplan, "Pastiche, Hyperbole, and the Composition of Jonah's Prayer," in *Petitioners, Penitents, and Poets: Prayer and Praying in Second Temple Times*, ed. Ariel Feldman and Timothy Sandoval, BZAW 524 (Berlin: De Gruyter, 2020), 27–42.

2. For details, see Rhiannon Graybill, John Kaltner, and Steven L. McKenzie, *Jonah: A New Translation with Commentary*, AYB 24H (New Haven/London: Yale University Press, 2023), 191–205. Ugarit was an ancient port city in what is now Syria. It flourished between 1400–1200 BCE when it was destroyed. Its ruins were discovered in 1928 and contained a large library of clay tablets, most written in the previously unknown language. The tablets are extremely important for Old Testament study because of their similarities to Hebrew and their accounts of Canaanite mythology.

3. See Amanda W. Benckhuysen, "Revisiting the Psalm of Jonah," *CTJ* 47 (2012): 5–31; and Ernst Wendland, "Song from the Seabed—How Sweet Does It Sound? Aspects of the Style, Structure, and Transmission of Jonah's Psalm," *Journal of Semitics* 11 (2002): 211–44. These recent treatments of the psalm by Benckhuysen and by Wendland focus on different aspects of its literary art. For more detailed treatments, see Magonet, *Form and Meaning*, and Uriel Simon יונה: *The Traditional Hebrew Text with the New JPS Translation*, JPSBC (Philadelphia: JPS, 1999), both somewhat dated but still eminently useful.

4. Simon, יונה, xxvi.

5. For example, Benckhuysen, "Revisiting the Psalm of Jonah," 7; Sasson, *Jonah*, 167; Wendland, "Song from the Seabed," 215, 218.

6. Maria Kassel, "Jonah: The Jonah Experience—For Women Too?" in *Feminist Biblical Interpretation: A Compendium of Critical Commentary on the Books of the Bible and Related Literature*, ed. Luise Schottroff, Marie-Theres Wacker, and Martin Rumscheidt (Grand Rapids: Eerdmans, 2012), 418–19; André LaCocque and Pierre-Emmanuel Lacocque, *Jonah: A Psycho-Religious Approach to the Prophet*, Studies in Personalities of the Old Testament (Columbia: University of South Carolina Press, 1990; repr. of *The Jonah Complex* [Atlanta: John Knox, 1981]), 56.

7. See esp. the studies of space in Jonah by Gert T. M. Prinsloo, "Place, Space and Identity in the Ancient Mediterranean World: Theory and Practice with Reference to the Book of Jonah," in *Constructions of Space V: Place, Space and Identity in the Ancient Mediterranean World*, ed. Gert T. M. Prinsloo and Christl M. Maier, LHBOTS 576 (New York: Bloomsbury T&T Clark, 2013), 3–24; and Anthony Rees, "Getting Up and Going Down: Towards a Spatial Poetics of Jonah," *The Bible and Critical Theory* 12 (2016): 40–48.

Chapter 5

1. For a representative example of this position, see Hans Walter Wolff, *Jonah: Church in Revolt* (St. Louis: Columbia Publishing House, 1978), 71–76.

2. Yvonne Sherwood, *A Biblical Text and Its Afterlives: The Survival of Jonah in Western Culture* (Cambridge University Press, 2000), 21–32.

3. Martin Luther, *Luther's Works. Vol. 19: Minor Prophets II: Jonah and Habakkuk*, ed. Hilton C. Oswald (St. Louis: Concordia, 1974), 91. On antisemitism in Augustine's view on Jonah, see Sherwood, *Biblical Text*, 22.

4. Chesung Justin Ryu, "Silence as Resistance: A Postcolonial Reading of the Silence of Jonah in Jonah 4.1–11," *Journal for the Study of the Old Testament* 34, no. 2 (2009): 195–218.

5. Uriel Simon, יונה: *The Traditional Hebrew Text with the New JPS Translation* (Philadelphia: Jewish Publication Society, 1999), xiii.

6. On midrash as a genre of Jewish biblical interpretation, see chapter 3.

7. *Mekhilta of Rabbi Ishmael*, 12.1.

8. *Mek. R. Ish.*, 1b–2a.

9. Thomas M. Bolin, *Freedom beyond Forgiveness: The Book of Jonah Re-Examined*, JSOTSup 236 (Sheffield: Sheffield Academic Press, 1997), 63.

10. Kenneth M. Craig, *A Poetics of Jonah: Art in the Service of Ideology* (Mercer University Press, 1999), 165.

11. See Yael Shemesh, "'And Many Beasts' (Jonah 4:11): The Function and Status of Animals in the Book of Jonah," *Journal of Hebrew Scriptures* 10 (2011); Willie Van Heerden, "Ecological Interpretations of the Jonah Narrative: Have They Succeeded in Overcoming Anthropocentrism?" *Journal of Semitics* 23, no. 1 (2014): 114–34; Jione Havea, *Jonah: An Earth Bible Commentary* (London: T&T Clark, 2020).

12. Donna J. Haraway, *The Companion Species Manifesto: Dogs, People, and Significant Otherness* (Chicago: Prickly Paradigm Press, 2003).

13. On comedy and the Book of Jonah, see the discussion of genre in chapter 3.

14. One line of argument holds that the fish saves Jonah from otherwise drowning in the sea. Another suggests that Jonah's thanksgiving is indeed for delivery from the fish; it is simply proleptically delivered.

15. We explore this further in chapter 4.

Chapter 6

1. André Lemaire, "Tarshish-*Tarsisi*: Problème de topographie historique biblique et assyrienne," in *Studies in Historical Geography and Biblical Historiography Presented to Zecharia Kallai*, ed. Gershon Galil and Moshe Weinfeld, VTSup 81 (Leiden: Brill, 2000), 44–47.

2. Several scholars have argued in favor of Tarsus as the site of Tarshish, including: Aurelio Padilla Monge, "Consideraciones sobre el Tarsis bíblico," *AuOr* 12 (1994): 66–70; Arie van der Kooij, *The Oracle*

of Tyre: The Septuagint of Isaiah XXIII as Version and Vision, VTSup 71 (Leiden: Brill, 1998), 40–47; and Reed Lessing, "Just Where Was Jonah Going? The Location of Tarshish in the Old Testament," *ConcJ* 28 (2002): 291–93.

3. Julia Montenegro and Arcadio del Castillo, "The Location of Tarshish: Critical Considerations," *RB* 123 (2016): 239–68.

4. John Day, "Where Was Tarshish?" in *Let Us Go Up to Zion: Essays in Honour of H. G. M. Williamson on the Occasion of His Sixty-Fifth Birthday*, ed. Iain Provan and Mark J. Boda, VTSup 153 (Leiden: Brill, 2012), 359–69.

5. As explained in chapter 2, we are using the NRSV numbering, which differs from the MT.

6. The connections between the story of Jonah and ancient Greek literature have long been noted, and a summary can be found in Lowell K. Handy, *Jonah's World: Social Science and the Reading of Prophetic Story* (London: Equinox, 2007), 83–89. The word for the fish in the Greek translation of the Bible is *ketos*, which is the basis for the English term *cetology*, which refers to the branch of zoology that studies whales, dolphins, and porpoises. This has likely contributed to the common view that the fish that swallowed Jonah was a whale. *Ketos* is the term that Greek sources use for these imaginary sea monsters, and it is also used by Jesus when he refers to the Jonah story (Matt 12:40).

7. This rabbinic interpretation is mentioned in James Limburg, *Jonah: A Commentary*, OTL (Louisville, KY: Westminster/John Knox, 1993), 110. See also, Yvonne Sherwood, *A Biblical Text and Its Afterlives: The Survival of Jonah in Western Culture* (Cambridge: Cambridge University Press, 2000), 117.

8. The work of the scholars mentioned in this paragraph can be found in Jack M. Sasson, *Jonah*, AYB 24B (New Haven/London: Yale, 1990), 156; Kevin J. Youngblood, *Jonah: God's Scandalous Mercy* (Grand Rapids, MI: Zondervan, 2014), 104; and Lena-Sofia Tiemeyer, "A New Look at the Biological Sex/Grammatical Gender of Jonah's Fish," *VT* 67 (2017): 315–23.

9. Among those who adopt this approach are John D. W. Watts, *The Books of Joel, Obadiah, Jonah, Nahum, Habakkuk and Zephaniah*, CBC (Cambridge: Cambridge University Press, 1975), 94; Daniel J. Simundson, *Hosea, Joel, Amos, Obadiah, Jonah, Micah*, AOTC (Nashville:

Abingdon, 2005), 282; and Phillip Cary, *Jonah*, BTCB (Grand Rapids, MI: Baker, 2008), 141.

10. Those who have seen Jonah 4:5 as an example of flashback include Leslie C. Allen, *The Books of Joel, Obadiah, Jonah and Malachi*, NICOT (Grand Rapids, MI: Eerdmans, 1976), 231; Douglas Stuart, *Hosea–Jonah*, WBC 31 (Waco, TX: Word, 1987), 499; and R. Reed Lessing, *Jonah*, ConcC (St. Louis: Concordia, 2007), 391.

11. A few scholars in recent years have proposed reading the final verse of the book as a statement or assertion rather than a question. See, e.g., Catherine L. Muldoon, *In Defense of Divine Justice: An Intertextual Approach to the Book of Jonah*, CBQMS 47 (Washington, DC: The Catholic Biblical Association of America, 2010), 140–49; and Amy Erickson, *Jonah: Introduction and Commentary*, Illuminations (Grand Rapids: Eerdmans, 2021), 407–14. We do not find these arguments to be persuasive.

12. For a treatment of Jonah and parody see William H. Hallo, "Jonah and the Uses of Parody," in *Thus Says the Lord: Essays on the Former and Latter Prophets in Honor of Robert R. Wilson*, ed. John J. Ahn and Stephen L. Cook (London: T&T Clark, 2009), 285–91.

13. More detail on these issues and other aspects of the book can be found in our commentary on Jonah: Rhiannon Graybill, John Kaltner, and Steven L. McKenzie, *Jonah*, AYB 24B (New Haven/London: Yale University Press, 2023).

Chapter 7

1. For fuller treatments of Jonah's reception history, see Yvonne Sherwood, *A Biblical Text and Its Afterlives: The Survival of Jonah in Western Culture* (Cambridge: Cambridge University Press, 2000); and Rhiannon Graybill, John Kaltner, and Steven L. McKenzie, *Jonah*, AYB 24B (New Haven/London: Yale University Press, 2023).

2. *Ba. Ta'nit*, 17a. Jack M. Sasson, *Jonah*, AYB 24B (New Haven/London: Yale, 1990), 159.

3. James Limburg, *Jonah: A Commentary*, OTL (Louisville, KY: Westminster/John Knox, 1993), 102.

4. *Pirqe Rabbi Eliezer*, 10. For an English translation, see Gerald Friedlander, *Pirkê de-Rabbi Eliezer (The Chapters of Rabbi Eliezer*

the Great): *According to the Text of the Manuscript Belonging to Abraham Epstein of Vienna* (London: Kegan Paul, Trench, Trubner, 1916), 69.

5. Limburg, *Jonah: A Commentary*, 111.

6. Limburg, *Jonah: A Commentary*, 112.

7. *Mekhilta, Pesichta Bo*, quoted in Meir Zlotowitz, *Jonah: A New Translation with a Commentary Anthologized from Talmudic, Midrashic and Rabbinic Sources*, 2nd ed. (New York: Mesorah, 1988), xxxiii.

8. Aryeh Wineman, *Mystic Tales from the Zohar* (Skokie, IL: Varda Books,1990), 58.

9. Jonathan Magonet, *Form and Meaning: Studies in Literary Techniques in the Book of Jonah* (Bern: Herbert Lang, 1976), 173.

10. For an extended discussion, see Simon Chow, *The Sign of Jonah Reconsidered: A Study of Its Meaning in the Gospel Traditions*, ConBNT 27 (Stockholm: Almqvist & Wiksell, 1995).

11. Hans Förster, "Jonah (Book and Person): New Testament," *EBR* 14, 572.

12. For example, James Swetnam argues that the sign in Matthew refers to Jonah's prophecy of destruction of Nineveh, paralleled by Jesus's prophecy of the destruction of Jerusalem, while for Luke, the sign is Jonah himself. See his "Some Signs of Jonah," *Bib* 68 (1987): 77. Chow (*Sign of Jonah*, 211–12) suggests that in Matthew, the sign refers to Jesus's death and resurrection, while in Luke it refers to the preaching of the Church, part of its larger mission.

13. Förster, "Jonah (Book and Person)," 572. Cf. Matt 12:10.

14. For a selection of these readings, a helpful and convenient resource is Alberto Ferreiro, ed., *The Twelve Prophets*, vol. 14 of *Ancient Christian Commentary on Scripture: Old Testament* (Downers Grove, IL: IVP Academic, 2003).

15. Tertullian, *The Resurrection of the Flesh*, 58; quoted in Ferreiro, *Twelve Prophets*, 139.

16. Sherwood, *Biblical Text*, 22.

17. Sherwood, *Biblical Text*, 22.

18. Martin Luther, *Minor Prophets II: Jonah and Habakkuk*, vol. 19 of *Luther's Works*, ed. Hilton C. Oswald (St. Louis: Concordia, 1974), 103–4.

19. A very good treatment of Jonah in written Islamic sources and artwork can be found in Robert C. Gregg, *Shared Stories, Rival Tellings:*

Early Encounters of Jews, Christians, and Muslims (Oxford/New York: Oxford University Press, 2015), 408–51.

20. For a more detailed discussion of how Jonah is interpreted differently in the Bible and the Qur'an, see John Kaltner and Christopher G. Frechette, *How the Qur'an Interprets the Bible: Comparing Islamic, Jewish, and Christian Scriptures* (Mahwah, NJ: Paulist Press, 2020), 160–74.

21. An English translation of al-Kisaʾi's account of Jonah's life is available in Muḥammad ibn ʿAbd Allāh al-Kisāʾī, *Tales of the Prophets*, trans. Wheeler M. Thackston Jr. (Chicago: KAZI Publications, 1997), 321–26.

22. Anthony Swindell, "Jonah: Literature," *EBR* 14 (2017): 588–92, here 589.

23. Herman Melville, *Moby-Dick*, ed. Hershel Parker and Harrison Hayford, Norton Critical Editions, 2nd ed.; New York: Norton, 2002 [1851]), 49.

24. Daniel Defoe, *Robinson Crusoe*, ed. Evan R. Davis (Ontario, Canada: Broadview Press, 2010 [1719]), 58.

25. Graham Huggan, "Last Whales: Eschatology, Extinction, and the Cetacean Imaginary in Winton and Pash," *Journal of Commonwealth Literature* 52, no. 2 (2017): 382–96.

26. Carlo Collodi, *The Adventures of Pinocchio: Story of a Puppet*, trans. Nicolas J. Perella (Berkeley: University of California Press, 1986).

27. Dietrich Bonhoeffer, *Letters and Papers from Prison* (Minneapolis, MN: Fortress Press 2010), 547–48.

28. See Gabriel Preil's "Then, Too, It Was Autumn" and "Jonah," and Dan Pagis's "Tidings," in David Curzon, ed., *Modern Poems on the Bible: An Anthology* (Philadelphia: The Jewish Publication Society, 1994), 255–57.

29. Norma Rosen, *Accidents of Influence: Writing as a Woman and a Jew in America* (Albany: SUNY Press, 1992), 87.

30. Adrienne Rich, "Yom Kippur 1984," in *Collected Poems: 1950–2012* (New York: Norton, 2016), 633–36; on Molodowksy, see Sol Liptzin, *Biblical Themes in World Literature* (Hoboken, NJ: Ktav Publishing House, Inc., 1985), 248–49; on Mankowitz, see Ellen Schiff, *From Stereotype to Metaphor: The Jew in Contemporary Drama*

(Albany: SUNY Press, 2012), 58–60; Joshua Max Feldman, *The Book of Jonah* (New York: Holt, 2014).

31. Robert Frost, *A Masque of Mercy* (New York: Holt, 1947).

32. Tony Kushner, *Angels in America: A Gay Fantasia on National Themes*, rev. and complete ed., 20th anniversary ed. (New York: Theatre Communications Group, 2013).

33. Zora Neale Hurston, *Jonah's Gourd Vine: A Novel* (New York: Harper & Row, 1990 [1934]).

34. Lucille Clifton, "jonah," in *Good Woman: Poems and a Memoir 1969–1980* (Brockport, NY: BOA Editions, 1987), 97.

35. See esp. Siobhán Dowling Long, "Jonah (Book and Person), Music," *EBR* 14 (2017), 595–97.

36. See the table in Graybill, Kaltner, and McKenzie, *Jonah*, 104–6.

37. Robert MacGimsey, track 10 on *Louis and the Good Book*, Decca Records, 1958.

38. William Travel, "Paul's Ministry," track A2 on Kitty Wells, *Singing on Sunday*, Decca Records, 1962; Roger Miller, "I Know Who It Is," track 2 on *The One and Only*, RCA Camden, 1965; Cy Coben, "Alphabet," track 7 on *Hank Snow Sings Sacred Songs*, RCA Victor, 1958.

39. Geoff Stephens and Don Black, "If You Believe," track 33 on Lena Horne, *The Lady and Her Music*, WEA Records, 1981; Lee Black and Kenna Turner West, "I Believe," track 1 on Gold City, *Pressed Down, Shaken Together, Running Over*, Daywind Records, 2001.

40. Author unknown; multiple artists and recordings.

41. Roger Martinez, "Fill This Place with Blood," track 12 on *Human Sacrifice*, Intense Records, 1988; Douglas Thieme, Larry Farkas, and Roger Martinez, "Out of the Will," track 9 on *Once Dead*, Intense Records, 1991; Roger Martinez, "Countless Corpses," track 6 on *Destruction Comes*, Frontline Records, 1989.

42. Fred Burch and Gerald Nelson, track 8 on *You'll Never Walk Alone*, RCA Camden, Presley, 1971.

43. Paul Simon, track 8 on *One Trick Pony*, Warner Brothers, 1980.

44. Bow Wow and Omarion, "Number Ones," track 9 on *Face Off*, Columbia, 2007.

45. Author unknown. Various artists and recordings.

46. Arthur Longbrake, aka Joe Arizonia, arranged by George Fairman, performed by Arthur Collins, Columbia, 1905.

47. Warner Chappell Music, Inc, BMG Rights Management, Downtown Music Publishing, Royalty Network, Raleigh Music Publishing.

48. Martin Gore, "The Love Thieves," track 2 on *Ultra*, Mute Records, Depeche Mode, 1997.

49. Kobi Farhi, Matti Svatizky, Uri Zelcha, Yossi Sassi, and Sami Bachar, track 11 on *Mabool: The Story of the Three Sons of Seven*, Century Media Records, 2004.

50. Elton John and Bernie Taupin, track 3 on *The Union*, Decca Records, 2010.

51. Stephen Ramsey and Martin Walkyier, Skyclad, "Terminus," track 10 on *The Wayward Sons of Mother Earth*, Noise International, 1991; Graham English and Martin Walkyier, "It Wasn't Meant to End This Way," track 11 on *Jonah's Ark*, Noise International, 1993.

52. Mark Myrie and Clement Dodd, "Murderer," track 3 on Buju Banton, *'Til Shiloh*, Island Records, 1995; Luciano, "Messenjah," track 1 on *Messenger*, Island Records, 1995.

53. Peter Gabriel, "Cuckoo Cocoon," track 4 on Genesis, *The Lion Lies Down on Broadway*, Charisma Records, 1974; Clifford Harris (aka T.I.), Jevon Hill, Michael Render, Theron Thomas, and Timothy Thomas, "Hallelujah," track 16 on T.I., *Trouble Man: Heavy Is the Head*, Grand Hustle Records, 2012.

54. J. B. Lenoir, "The Whale Has Swallowed Me," recorded by various artists; Guster, "Jonah," track 14 on *Easy Wonderful*, Republic Records, 2010.

55. Written by Harold Arlen and Johnny Mercer, 1944; recorded by various artists.

56. David Glasper and Marcus Lillington, "Jonah," track 1 on Breathe, *All that Jazz*, A&M, 1988; Lisa Walker, "Jonah," track 6 on Wussy, *Left for Dead*, Shake It Records, 2007.

57. An image of the Huqoq Synagogue mosaic can be seen at https://www.nationalgeographic.com/culture/article/jonah-tower-babel-huqoq-ancient-synagogue-mosaic.

58. Images of the sarcophagus and its individual scenes are available at https://www.christianiconography.info/sicily/sarcophagusJonah.html.

59. This painting can be viewed at https://www.metmuseum.org/art/collection/search/453683.

60. See https://www.wga.hu/frames-e.html?/html/t/tintoret/3b/2upper/1/07jonah.html.

61. See https://thejewishmuseum.org/collection/26645-jonah.

62. See https://americanart.si.edu/artwork/jonah-21449.

63. See https://emuseum.nasher.duke.edu/objects/6480/jonah-and-the-whale;jsessionid=4F9EA7DF7D8DF939AAC3C4EAE399E31C?ctx=c7652a1e-1d20-492b-a782-a5c3494f0654.

64. See dennismcgeary.com.

65. See https://debbiechavers.blogspot.com/2011/04/jonah-gone-fishing.html.

Bibliography

Abrams, M. H. *A Glossary of Literary Terms.* New York: Holt, Rinehart & Winston, 1981.

Allen, Leslie C. *The Books of Joel, Obadiah, Jonah and Malachi.* NICOT. Grand Rapids, MI: Eerdmans, 1976.

Band, Arnold J. "Swallowing Jonah: The Eclipse of Parody." *Prooftexts* 10, no. 2 (1990): 177–95.

Benckhuysen, Amanda W. "Revisiting the Psalm of Jonah." *CTJ* 47 (2012): 5–31.

Ben Zvi, Ehud. *Signs of Jonah: Reading and Rereading in Ancient Yehud.* JSOTSup 367. London: Sheffield Academic Press/Continuum, 2003.

———. "Twelve Prophetic Books or 'The Twelve': A Few Preliminary Considerations." In *Forming Prophetic Literature: Essays on Isaiah and the Twelve in Honor of John D. W. Watts*, edited by James W. Watts and Paul R. House, 125–56. JSOTSup 235. Sheffield: Sheffield Academic Press, 1996.

Bewer, Julius A. *A Critical and Exegetical Commentary on Jonah.* ICC. Edinburgh: T&T Clark, 1912.

Bolin, Thomas M. *Freedom beyond Forgiveness: The Book of Jonah Re-Examined.* JSOTSup 236. Sheffield: Sheffield Academic Press, 1997.

Bonhoeffer, Dietrich. *Letters and Papers from Prison.* Minneapolis, MN: Fortress Press, 2010.

Cary, Phillip. *Jonah.* BTCB. Grand Rapids, MI: Baker, 2008.

Chow, Simon. *The Sign of Jonah Reconsidered: A Study of Its Meaning in the Gospel Traditions.* ConBNT 27. Stockholm: Almqvist & Wiksell, 1995.

Clifton, Lucille. *Good Woman: Poems and a Memoir 1969–1980.* Brockport, NY: BOA Editions, 1987.

Collodi, Carlo. *The Adventures of Pinocchio: Story of a Puppet.* Translated by Nicolas J. Perella. Berkeley: University of California Press, 1986.

Craig, Kenneth M. *A Poetics of Jonah: Art in the Service of Ideology.* Macon, GA: Mercer University Press, 1999.

Curzon, David, ed. *Modern Poems on the Bible: An Anthology.* Philadelphia: The Jewish Publication Society, 1994.

Day, John. "Where Was Tarshish?" In *Let Us Go Up to Zion: Essays in Honour of H. G. M. Williamson on the Occasion of his Sixty-Fifth Birthday*, edited by Iain Provan and Mark J. Boda, 359–69. VTSup 153. Leiden: Brill, 2012.

Defoe, Daniel. *Robinson Crusoe.* Edited by Evan R. Davis. Ontario, Canada: Broadview Press, 2010 [1719].

Eagleton, Terry. "J. L. Austin and the Book of Jonah." *New Blackfriars* 69, no. 815 (1988).

Edelman, Diana V. "Jonah among the Twelve in the MT: The Triumph of Torah over Prophecy." In *The Production of Prophecy: Constructing Prophecy and Prophets in Yehud*, edited by Diana V. Edelman and Ehud Ben Zvi, 150–67. London/New York: Routledge, 2014.

Erickson, Amy. *Jonah: Introduction and Commentary.* Illuminations. Grand Rapids: Eerdmans, 2021.

Feldman, Joshua Max. *The Book of Jonah.* New York: Holt, 2014.

Ferreiro, Alberto, ed. *The Twelve Prophets.* Vol. 14, *Ancient Christian Commentary on Scripture: Old Testament.* Downers Grove, IL: IVP Academic, 2003.

Förster, Hans. "Jonah (Book and Person): New Testament." *EBR* 14, 572.

Friedlander, Gerald. *Pirkê de Rabbi Eliezer (The Chapters of Rabbi Eliezer the Great): According to the Text of the Manuscript Belonging to Abraham Epstein of Vienna.* London: Kegan Paul, Trench, Trübner, 1916.

Frost, Robert. *A Masque of Mercy.* New York: Holt, 1947.

Gaines, Janet Howe. *Forgiveness in a Wounded World: Jonah's Dilemma.* Atlanta: Society of Biblical Literature, 2003.

Garber, Zev, and Bruce Zuckerman, "The Odd Prophet Out and In." In *Lemaʾan Ziony: Essays in Honor of Ziony Zevit*, edited by Frederick E. Greenspahn and Gary A. Rendsburg, 175–202. Eugene, OR: Cascade, 2017.

Graybill, Rhiannon, John Kaltner, and Steven L. McKenzie. *Jonah: A New Translation with Commentary.* AYB 24H. New Haven/London: Yale University Press, 2023.

Green, Barbara. *Jonah's Journeys.* Interfaces. Collegeville, MN: Liturgical Press, 2005.

Gregg, Robert C. *Shared Stories, Rival Tellings: Early Encounters of Jews, Christians, and Muslims.* Oxford/New York: Oxford University Press, 2015.

Hallo, William H. "Jonah and the Uses of Parody." In *Thus Says the Lord: Essays on the Former and Latter Prophets in Honor of Robert R. Wilson*, ed. John J. Ahn and Stephen L. Cook, 285–91. London: T&T Clark, 2009.

Handy, Lowell K. *Jonah's World: Social Science and the Reading of Prophetic Story.* London: Equinox, 2007.

Haraway, Donna J. *The Companion Species Manifesto: Dogs, People, and Significant Otherness.* Chicago: Prickly Paradigm Press, 2003.

Havea, Jione. *Jonah: An Earth Bible Commentary.* London: T&T Clark, 2020.

Huggan, Graham. "Last Whales: Eschatology, Extinction, and the Cetacean Imaginary in Winton and Pash." *Journal of Commonwealth Literature* 52, no. 2 (2017): 382–96.

Hurston, Zora Neale. *Jonah's Gourd Vine: A Novel.* New York: Harper & Row, 1990 [1934].

Kaltner, John, and Christopher G. Frechette, *How the Qur'an Interprets the Bible: Comparing Islamic, Jewish, and Christian Scriptures.* Mahwah, NJ: Paulist Press, 2020.

Kaplan, Jonathan. "Pastiche, Hyperbole, and the Composition of Jonah's Prayer." In *Petitioners, Penitents, and Poets: Prayer and Praying in Second Temple Times*, edited by Ariel Feldman and Timothy Sandoval, 27–42. BZAW 524. Berlin: De Gruyter, 2020.

Kassel, Maria. "Jonah: The Jonah Experience—for Women Too?" In *Feminist Biblical Interpretation: A Compendium of Critical Commentary on the Books of the Bible and Related Literature*, edited by Luise Schottroff, Marie-Theres Wacker, and Martin Rumscheidt, 411–20. Grand Rapids: Eerdmans, 2012.

Kisā'ī, Muḥammad ibn 'Abd Allāh al-. *Tales of the Prophets*. Translated by Wheeler M. Thackston Jr. Chicago: KAZI Publications, 1997.

Kooij, Arie van der. *The Oracle of Tyre: The Septuagint of Isaiah XXIII as Version and Vision*. VTSup 71. Leiden: Brill, 1998.

Kushner, Tony. *Angels in America: A Gay Fantasia on National Themes*. 20th anniversary ed. New York: Theatre Communications Group, 2013.

LaCocque, André, and Pierre-Emmanuel Lacocque. *Jonah: A Psycho-Religious Approach to the Prophet*. Columbia: University of South Carolina Press, 1990. Reprint of *The Jonah Complex*. Atlanta: John Knox, 1981.

Landes, George M. "Jonah: A *Māšāl*?" In *Israelite Wisdom: Theological and Literary Essays in Honor of Samuel Terrien*, edited by Samuel L. Terrien and John G. Gammie, 137–58. Missoula, MT: Scholars Press for Union Theological Seminary, 1978.

Lemaire, André. "Tarshish-*Tarsisi:* Problème de topographie historique biblique et assyrienne." In *Studies in Historical Geography and Biblical Historiography Presented to Zecharia Kallai*, edited by Gershon Galil and Moshe Weinfeld, 44–47. VTSup 81. Leiden: Brill, 2000.

Lessing, Reed. *Jonah*. ConcC. St. Louis: Concordia, 2007.

―――. "Just Where Was Jonah Going? The Location of Tarshish in the Old Testament." *ConcJ* 28, no. 3 (2002): 291–93.

Limburg, James. *Jonah: A Commentary*. OTL. Louisville, KY: Westminster/John Knox, 1993.

Liptzin, Sol. *Biblical Themes in World Literature*. Hoboken: Ktav Publishing House, 1985.

Long, Siobhán Dowling. "Jonah (Book and Person), Music." *EBR* 14 (2017): 595–97.

Luther, Martin. *Luther's Works. Vol. 19: Minor Prophets II: Jonah and Habakkuk*. Edited by Hilton C. Oswald. St. Louis: Concordia, 1974.

Magonet, Jonathan. *Form and Meaning: Studies in Literary Techniques in the Book of Jonah*. Bern: Herbert Lang, 1976.

Marcus, David. *From Balaam to Jonah: Anti-Prophetic Satire in the Hebrew Bible*. Atlanta: Scholars Press, 1995.

Mather, Judson. "The Comic Art of the Book of Jonah." *Soundings: An Interdisciplinary Journal* 65, no. 3 (1982): 280–91.

McKenzie, Steven L., Rhiannon Graybill, and John Kaltner. "Underwater Archaeology: The Compositional Layers of the Book of Jonah." *VT* 70, no. 1 (2020): 83–103.

Melville, Herman. *Moby-Dick.* Edited by Hershel Parker and Harrison Hayford. 2nd ed. New York: Norton, 2002 [1851].

Miles, John A. "Laughing at the Bible: Jonah as Parody." *JQR* 65, no. 3 (1975): 168–81.

Montenegro, Julia, and Arcadio del Castillo. "The Location of Tarshish: Critical Considerations." *RB* 123 (2016): 239–68.

Muldoon, Catherine L. *In Defense of Divine Justice: An Intertextual Approach to the Book of Jonah.* CBQMS 47. Washington, DC: Catholic Biblical Association of America, 2010.

Nogalski, James D. *The Book of the Twelve: Hosea–Jonah.* SHBC. Macon, GA: Smyth & Helwys, 2011.

———. *Redactional Processes in the Book of the Twelve.* BZAW 218. Berlin/New York: De Gruyter, 1993.

Padilla Monge, Aurelio. "Consideraciones sobre el Tarsis bíblico." *AuOr* 12 (1994): 66–70.

Pajunen, Mika S., and Hanne von Weissenberg. "The Book of Malachi, Manuscript 4Q76 (4QXII[a]), and the Formation of the 'Book of the Twelve.'" *JBL* 134 (2015): 731–51.

Person, Raymond F. *In Conversation with Jonah: Conversation Analysis, Literary Criticism, and the Book of Jonah.* JSOTSup 220. Sheffield: Sheffield Academic Press, 1996.

Prinsloo, Gert T. M. "Place, Space and Identity in the Ancient Mediterranean World: Theory and Practice with Reference to the Book of Jonah." In *Constructions of Space V: Place, Space and Identity in the Ancient Mediterranean World*, edited by Gert T. M. Prinsloo and Christl M. Maier, 3–24. LHBOTS 576. New York: Bloomsbury T&T Clark, 2013.

Rees, Anthony. "Getting Up and Going Down: Towards a Spatial Poetics of Jonah." *The Bible and Critical Theory* 12 (2016): 40–48.

Rich, Adrienne. *Collected Poems: 1950–2012.* New York: Norton, 2016.

Rofé, Alexander. "Classes in the Prophetical Stories: Didactic Legend and Parable." In *Congress Volume*, edited by J. A. Emerton, 52–170. VTSup 26. Leiden: Brill, 1974.

Rosen, Norma. *Accidents of Influence: Writing as a Woman and a Jew in America.* Albany: SUNY Press, 1992.

Ryu, Chesung Justin. "Silence as Resistance: A Postcolonial Reading of the Silence of Jonah in Jonah 4.1–11." *Journal for the Study of the Old Testament* 34, no. 2 (2009): 195–218.

Sasson, Jack M. *Jonah.* AYB 24B. New York: Doubleday, 1990.

Schart, Aaron. "The Jonah-Narrative within the Book of the Twelve." In *Perspectives on the Formation of the Book of the Twelve*, edited by Rainer Albertz, James D. Nogalski, and Jakob Wöhrle, 109–28. BZAW 433. Berlin/New York: De Gruyter, 2012.

Schiff, Ellen. *From Stereotype to Metaphor: The Jew in Contemporary Drama.* Albany: SUNY Press, 2012.

Shemesh, Yael. "'And Many Beasts' (Jonah 4:11): The Function and Status of Animals in the Book of Jonah." *Journal of Hebrew Scriptures* 10 (2010).

Sherwood, Yvonne. *A Biblical Text and Its Afterlives: The Survival of Jonah in Western Culture.* Cambridge: Cambridge University Press, 2000.

Simon, Uriel. יונה: *The Traditional Hebrew Text with the New JPS Translation.* JPSBCJ. Philadelphia: JPS, 1999.

Simundson, Daniel J. *Hosea, Joel, Amos, Obadiah, Jonah, Micah.* AOTC. Nashville: Abingdon, 2005.

Spronk, Klass. "Jonah, Nahum, and the Book of the Twelve: A Response to Jakob Wöhrle." *JHebS* 9 (2009).

Stuart, Douglas. *Hosea-Jonah.* WBC 31. Waco, TX: Word, 1987.

Sweeney, Marvin A. "Sequence and Interpretation in the Book of the Twelve." In *Reading and Hearing the Book of the Twelve*, edited by James D. Nogalski and Marvin A. Sweeney, 52–170. SymS 15. Atlanta: Society of Biblical Literature, 2000.

———. "Synchronic and Diachronic Concerns in Reading the Book of the Twelve Prophets." In *Perspectives on the Formation of the Book of the Twelve*, edited by Rainer Albertz, James D. Nogalski, and Jakob Wöhrle, 25–30. BZAW 433. Berlin/New York: De Gruyter, 2012.

Swetnam, James. "Some Signs of Jonah." *Bib* 68 (1987).

Swindell, Anthony. "Jonah: Literature." *EBR* 14 (2017): 588–92.

Syren, Roger. "The Book of Jonah—a Reversed Diasporanovella?" *SEÅ* 58 (1993): 7–14.

Thomas, D. Winton. "A Consideration of Some Unusual Ways of Expressing the Superlative in Hebrew." *VT* 3 (1950): 209–24.

Tiemeyer, Lena-Sofia. "A New Look at the Biological Sex/Grammatical Gender of Jonah's Fish." *VT* 67 (2017): 315–23.

Trible, Phyllis L. *Rhetorical Criticism: Context, Method, and the Book of Jonah.* Guides to Biblical Scholarship. Minneapolis, MN: Fortress Press, 1994.

———. "Studies in the Book of Jonah." PhD Diss., Columbia University, 1963.

Van Heerden, Willie. "Ecological Interpretations of the Jonah Narrative: Have They Succeeded in Overcoming Anthropocentrism?" *Journal for Semitics* 23, no. 1 (2014): 114–34.

Watts, John D. W. *The Books of Joel, Obadiah, Jonah, Nahum, Habakkuk and Zephaniah.* CBC. Cambridge: Cambridge University Press, 1975.

Wendland, Ernst. "Song from the Seabed—How Sweet Does It Sound? Aspects of the Style, Structure and Transmission of Jonah's Psalm." *Journal for Semitics* 11, no. 2 (2002): 211–44.

Wineman, Aryeh. *Mystic Tales from the Zohar.* Skokie, IL: Varda Books, 1990.

Wöhrle, Jakob. "A Prophetic Reflection on Divine Forgiveness: The Integration of the Book of Jonah into the Book of the Twelve." *JHebS* 9 (2009).

Youngblood, Kevin J. *Jonah: God's Scandalous Mercy.* Grand Rapids, MI: Zondervan, 2014.

Zlotowitz, Meir. *Jonah: A New Translation with a Commentary Anthologized from Talmudic, Midrashic and Rabbinic Sources.* 2nd ed. New York: Mesorah, 1988.

Also in the WATSA Series

**What Are
They Saying
About Luke?**
3111-0 $14.95
160 pp.

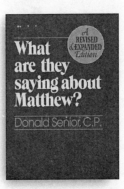

> **What Are They
> Saying About
> Matthew?**
> 3624-4 $12.95
> 144 pp.

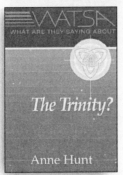

**What Are They
Saying About
Scripture
and Ethics?
Rev. ed.**
3609-0 $14.95
160 pp.

> **What Are They
> Saying About
> the Formation
> of Pauline
> Churches?**
> 3768-2 $12.95
> 144 pp.

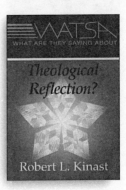

**What Are
They Saying
About the
Trinity?**
3806-9 $11.95
104 pp.

> **What Are They
> Saying About
> Theological
> Reflection?**
> 3968-5 $10.95
> 120 pp.

Also in the WATSA Series

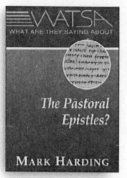

What Are They Saying About the Pastoral Epistles?
3975-8 $12.95
160 pp.

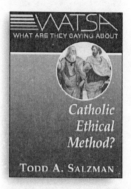

What Are They Saying About Catholic Ethical Method?
4159-0 $14.95
192 pp.

What Are They Saying About New Testament Apocalyptic?
4228-7 $12.95
128 pp.

What Are They Saying About Mark?
4263-5 $12.95
112 pp.

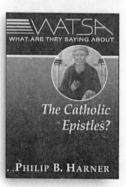

What Are They Saying About the Catholic Epistles?
4188-4 $12.95
144 pp.

What Are They Saying About John?
Rev. ed.
4337-2 $14.95
192 pp.